American Women and Political Participation

American Women and Political Participation

THE IMPACTS OF WORK, GENERATION, AND FEMINISM

Karen Beckwith

CONTRIBUTIONS IN WOMEN'S STUDIES, NUMBER 68
Greenwood Press
NEW YORK
WESTPORT, CONNECTICUT
LONDON

Library of Congress Cataloging-in-Publication Data

Beckwith, Karen, 1950–
  American women and political participation.

  (Contributions in women's studies, ISSN 0147-104X ;
no. 68)
  Bibliography: p.
  Includes index.
  1. Women in politics—United States. 2. Women—
United States—Political activity. 3. Feminism—
United States. I. Title. II. Series.
HQ1391.U5B43 1986   305.4'2'0973   85-27284
ISBN 0-313-24507-X (lib. bdg. : alk. paper)

Library of Congress Catalog Card Number: 85-27284
ISBN: 0-313-24507-X
ISSN: 0147-104X

First published in 1986

Greenwood Press, Inc.
88 Post Road West, Westport, Connecticut 06881

Printed in the United States of America

The paper used in this book complies with the
Permanent Paper Standard issued by the National
Information Standards Organization (Z39.48-1984).

10 9 8 7 6 5 4 3 2 1

For Fitz Beckwith Collings and John Russell Collings

CONTENTS

TABLES

ACKNOWLEDGMENTS

There are many people I wish to acknowledge and thank for their support and guidance while I was struggling to understand women's mass-level political participation and its sources. Several friends who are Women's Studies scholars or female members of the academic community made indirect but crucial contributions to this work. I wish to express my enduring gratitude to Sari Knopp Biklen; Josephine Donovan (my first—and only—Women's Studies professor); Miriam Golden; Helen Graves (my first female departmental colleague); Mary Fainsod Katzenstein; Susan Marie Olson; and Doris Marie Provine. I am also grateful to Thomas E. Patterson, Robert D. McClure, Philip Beardsley, James E. Campbell, and William Provine, who provided guidance and assistance in the early days of my work. R. Darcy, a friend of many years' standing, read the manuscript on short notice and returned it with valuable criticisms, copies of relevant articles, and advice on child-rearing. I thank all of these friends and colleagues profusely but admit, of course, that any errors of fact or interpretation herein rest with me alone.

The completion of this work was possible through the generous and efficient support of the College of Wooster, whose Vice-President for Academic Affairs Donald Harward and former Dean of the Faculty Vivian Holliday provided me with a computer terminal, computer time, copying facilities, and general support funds. My colleagues in the Department of Political Science were supportive and encouraging of my work. William Baird of the Economics Department provided access to the data from the University of Michigan's Inter-University Consortium for Political and Social Research. Neither the original collectors of the data nor the Consortium bear any responsibility for the analyses or interpretations presented here. Arnold Grossblatt, Lee Schultz, and Carl Zimmerman, of the College Computer Center, provided me with expert advice and assistance; they were generous with their time, and I am very grateful to them. The "Friends of Feminist Theory" group at the College provided me with the intellectual setting possible for the consideration of several issues presented in Chapter I of this work. I thank these colleagues at the College for providing both general and particular encouragement for research and intellectual endeavor and am grateful to the College for providing a supportive scholarly atmosphere.

I am indebted in many personal ways to my parents, siblings, spouse, and friends. I could not have finished this book without their help, and I am profoundly grateful to each and all of them. I owe special thanks to my new friend and wonderful neighbor Julie Vizzo, who provided tolerance, a fine sense of humor and emergency childcare while I worked on this book. Marilyn and Charles Beckwith, my parents, provided several weeks' worth of round-the-clock childcare for my son, Fitz Beckwith Collings, supported by a cadre of Fitz's expert aunts and uncles: Sally Ann Beckwith, Kathleen Kline Beckwith, Mark Andrew Beckwith, and John Clayton Beckwith. (But of all the family childcare assistants, the greatest of these are my mother Marilyn, and Sally.) Sally Ann Beckwith also provided emergency library research assistance for me. Cathy Beckwith Laube helped proofread the manuscript. And somehow, John Russell Collings, my husband, managed to commute weekly from Detroit, "to defend the workers' interests," and to be a parent to our child and a wise and steadfast support to me.

It is to John Russell Collings and Fitz Beckwith Collings that I dedicate this work: to Fitz, for reminding me constantly of the tensions between being a mother and being a scholar and of the necessity for constructing new ways of being both; and to John, for reminding me that the construction of those new ways is possible.

American Women
and Political
Participation

CHAPTER I

WOMEN AND POLITICAL PARTICIPATION: AN INTRODUCTION AND SOME CONSIDERATIONS

This study was prompted by two interests dominant in my academic and political lives: a concern about mass-level political participation and a commitment to feminism. These interests drove me to read, as an undergraduate in the early 1970s, probably every published work on women and political participation (of which there were few), as well as those on feminist theory. I was struck at the time by the paucity of research in all subfields of women's studies scholarship—a new, or at least newly rediscovered, academic discipline,—but especially by the lack of study of women's mass-level political participation, which at the time even included voting behavior. Most of the scholarship on women and politics in the last decade focused upon the political behavior of female elites.[1] This is not terribly surprising—nor was it surprising then, given that it is still within the scope of scholars to study the *universe* of female national legislators in the United States. What research had been published on women's mass-level participation was limited in the following ways. First, it focused on electoral behavior (voting, discussing the campaign with others, and interest and involvement in presidential campaigns).

Second, it pointed to large and significant differences between men and women in turnout.[2] Even much of the more recent research is concerned with these differences in mass-level participation between women and men. Berenice Carroll pointed out in 1979 that the major fact of women's political participation is how *little* it differs from that of men at the mass level. She writes:

. . . the picture which emerges is not one of marginality but of women holding political attitudes and engaging in political behaviors very similar to those
of men, at all levels from school children to party activists and officeholders.
On almost all measures of voting, participation, efficacy, activism, ideology,
and performance, sex differences between men and women, if present at all,
are small. This appears to be true for both masses and for "elites"—party
leaders and activists. The similarities between male and female political behavior extend into the general population and are small in the whole range of
political activities including voting, grass roots participation, attitudes, protest
activities, traditional party work, etc.[3]

The evidence cited by Carroll for minor differences between men and
women raises again the unanswered question of Susan Bourque and
Jean Grossholtz: "If there is little evidence of differences between
men and women on certain measures of participation, how does one
account for the fact that men dominate political life?"[4] We will discuss the extent to which gender related differences in mass-level participation exist in Chapter II.

Third, this literature assumed that "male" behavior was the standard of citizenship by which female participation should be judged,[5]
and it assumed that the sources of men's participation in politics were
universal: occupation and education being the primary resources for
participation in politics.

This study is the culmination of my understanding of the early literature on women's political participation at the mass level and an
attempt to do two things: first, to investigate and present the differences in women's and men's political participation in their various
forms at the mass level; and second, to examine the sources of wom-
en's political behavior that may be unique to women. In this way, I
hoped to examine a broad range of mass-level political participation,
going beyond the traditional focus on voting behavior[6] to investigate
forms of political participation that might be more likely on their face
to include women as participants. There are difficulties in so doing,
given the emphasis in national political surveys on electoral participation and, perhaps, the reality that nonelectoral forms of political participation may require that evidence be collected in a manner other
than such national studies.

Second, I have sought to go beyond the examination of standard
variables associated with political participation, such as occupation and
education, to ask what those variables mean to *women* and to examine

other variables that may have considerable impact on women's ability to be politically active.

This study is organized around these two major concerns: the extent to which male and female participation rates differ and the ways in which the life experiences of women—their work, their exposure to feminist movements, their support for feminist ideology—affect their political behavior. Chapter II of this work addresses this first concern, using the data from the ICPSR (Michigan's Inter-University Consortium for Political and Social Research) American National Election Studies from 1952 to 1976 to examine the bivariate relationship between political behavior and gender—to see what the "simple" differences are.

It does not give away too much of the plot at this point to state that, by and large, gender differences in political participation are few and modest and that this has been the case, rather than the exception, since the early 1950s. There are several works which suggest, if not that gender differences in participation are small, at least that "sex"[7] is not a major variable in explaining participation. Sandra Baxter and Marjorie Lansing, for example, argue that "simply looking at gender as *the* determinant of turnout is unwise. . . . The combination of gender with educational level, employment status and occupation, income level and region does lead to better understanding and more accurate predictions of voting."[8] They found education the single most important factor related to turnout for both men and women, writing: "Education will time and time again prove valuable in the understanding of political attitudes and behaviors other than voting."[9] Raymond Wolfinger and Steven Rosenstone confirm this claim in *Who Votes?*, finding that there are virtually no differences in turnout between women and men until the age of forty, and that "[n]early all the differences in turnout between older men and women is accounted for by differences in other demographic variables."[10]

Given this, the remainder of this work focuses on the issue of women's life experiences and the extent to which the ways that women find themselves situated, differently from men, encourage or discourage political participation. Certainly one of the best and most thoroughly documented claims about American women is that our lives differ from those of men—even from those of men with whom we live in intimate, everyday contact. As women, we have primary, and sometimes exclusive, responsibility for children and childcare and for housework;

when we work for wages outside the home, we work in occupations where women predominate (although not necessarily where we dominate), where the character of the work reflects in many ways our work in households, where chances of promotion or increased responsibility are meager, and where the pay and benefits are poor. Our lives also differ from those of men in terms of the mobilization of feminist movements—how we relate to them as women[11] and how successful feminist movements transform the conditions of our lives. Chapter III focuses on the issue of women's work and political participation by examining variables appropriate to the working lives of women: women's unpaid employment within the home and/or our employment outside the home for wages, women's income, and childcare. Chapter IV examines the extent to which women, witnessing the example of—or even being part of—a feminist movement, are able to draw upon that experience, in a way which men do not, to increase their political participation. In Chapter V, we examine the extent to which support for feminist issues helps individual women mobilize for political action.

While occupation and education have been major variables for predicting political participation, antecedent variables such as race and class also appear throughout participation literature.[12] Certainly, unraveling the impacts of gender, race, and class upon participation remains a major question for political behavior scholars. This work does not concern itself with such untangling, but it does attempt a consideration of the impacts of race and class upon women's political participation. To what extent does the fact of being black or of identifying oneself as "working class" affect a woman's political participation, and do these two "facts"—of race and class—affect women differently than men? Chapter VI is an initial attempt to answer these two questions, and therein are presented data on women's and men's political participation, stratified by race and class. Chapter VII concludes this work.

The data base employed throughout this study is the American National Election Studies from the Inter-University Consortium for Political and Social Research at the University of Michigan, for the years 1952 to 1976. By examining the data for this twenty-four-year time span, we have sufficient information on long-term patterns and trends in women's political participation and its sources; by focusing on the postwar period, we include a decade during which no feminist movement existed (roughly, 1952 to 1963) and another decade during which the feminist movement was initiated, developed, and impressively successful (1963 to 1976). By ending our examination of women's political participation in 1976, we allow ourselves the advantage of avoiding a consideration of the rise of an intense, anti-feminist minority and the confounding effects of the conservative Reagan administration and its opposition to women's rights.[13] Before 1980, both major political parties supported ratification of the Equal Rights Amendment; there was—and still is—strong majority support for women's issues; and there was no discernible difference in the vote choices of women and men. The question of whether the presence of a frankly anti-feminist administration and an intense, anti-feminist minority movement depresses women's political participation is an important one, but its answer is outside the scope of this study.[14]

Before we turn to the consideration of gender related differences in political participation in Chapter II, it may be worth the time to pause here and consider the importance of understanding how—or whether—women's unique social location may yield an equally unique female politics. Berenice Carroll, for example, reminds us of "Jane Jaquette's call for political scientists . . . to look more carefully at the "private" sphere rather than focus on the conventionally defined "public" or "political" sphere, and to give more attention to women's small-group behavior and the 'politics of everyday life.' "[15]

Temma Kaplan attempts this in her focus on female collective action in Barcelona in the early 1900s, arguing that many studies "ignore other forms of associational life in the family, the church, workers' circles, cooperatives, and women's groups. Mass support, particularly from women, comes precisely from such organizations."[16]

Kaplan investigates how "female consciousness," which results from "the deep-rooted, age-old experience of women in giving and preserving life, nurturing and sustaining,"[17] can lead to women's struggle to defend "the rights accorded to them by the sexual division of labor"[18]—child rearing, the preservation of life—giving evidence to a politics rooted in women's unique situation. She explains:

To do the work society assigns them, women have pursued social rather than narrowly political goals. When it appears that the survival of the community is at stake, women activate their networks to fight anyone—left or right, male or female—who they think interferes with their ability to preserve life as they know it.[19]

The consciousness which gives rise to this political activism, according to Kaplan, is conservative but contains "profoundly radical political implications."[20] While this work cannot focus on a uniquely female brand of politics which emanates from "female consciousness," nonetheless we will attempt to examine—using survey data, large nationally representative samples, and seven data years—the extent to which women's political participation has different motive forces, based on their different location(s) in society in the United States; and we will come to some conclusions rather different from those of Kaplan.

I raise the point of Kaplan's very intriguing work here—and that of others—in an attempt to fit my own work into the context of political theory developed by a variety of feminist scholars in the last decade. The lack of connection between feminist theory and feminist empirical research has been well noted by Berenice Carroll, who writes:

One is struck by a sharp disjunction between the academic writings, on one hand, and the Marxist or radical writings on the other. This disjunction is marked not only by the difference in point of view but by an almost total absence of communication. Neither the mainstream writers in academic journals nor the feminist radicals take any notice of each other's work, even where they seem to overlap in topical interest. . . . [21]

Replacing Carroll's categories of "academic" and "radical" with "empirical scholars" and "theorists," it seems accurate that there is less intellectual exchange between the two groups than feminist scholars might wish, since certainly the creation of good theory rests in part on an understanding of the empirical data and just as certainly good empirical research relies on the guidance of feminist theory pointing to the valuable, crucial questions for research. One example of the rejection of this claim is the admission by Baxter and Lansing, in their most recent (1983) edition of *Women and Politics*: "Readers looking for the 'theory' tested in this book will be disappointed, for there is little. The topic of women and politics is too new for much theory-building and theory-testing research to have been done."[22]

This work attempts an empirical test, in a very limited way, of the claims, outlined above, that women's unique social location leads to unique motivations for women's political participation. It is an attempt to meet the challenge recognized by Michelle Rosaldo: ''to provide new ways of linking the particulars of women's lives, activities, and goals to inequalities wherever they exist.'' [23] In ''linking the particulars of women's lives,'' we need to avoid overstating and romanticizing women's experiences as mothers and sustainers of life, while recognizing the potential political implications of such linkages (whether positive or negative); we need to sustain a tenuous balance between affirming women's unique social locations and becoming mired in a focus on the ''angel of the hearth,'' to the exclusion of understandings of cross-class and cross-race differences among women. And while feminist theorists need to avoid sentimentalizing motherhood,[24] empirical scholars must remember that social constructions such as ''mother'' and ''wife'' entail certain kinds of experience which may be the source for uniquely ''female'' political participation—whether in its motivations, its forms, its contents, or its goals.[25] With these numerous caveats in mind, and with the humbling acknowledgment that meeting all of these various conditions for research on women and politics is formidable if not impossible, we turn to an examination of women's mass-level political participation.

POSSIBLE EXPLANATIONS OF FEMALE PARTICIPATION

It is the purpose of this work to examine the political participation of women in the United States in the past quarter century: to assess the types of participation in which American women have been engaged, the pattern of American women's participation across that time span, and the sources of that participation which are unique to women's experience. While there are some explanations of political participation that are generally understood as the shared and similar experience of both women and men—education, political interest, class, and race, there are others which are peculiar to women which have not been examined. Life experiences in the United States vary by gender and, in an assessment of gender related differences in political participation, an evaluation of how these life experiences affect participation is necessary. It is because of the known gender related differences in employment socialization, family roles, and other experiences that gender becomes an important political variable.

There are three major considerations about women's political participation that this study considers. First, to what extent does woman's work restrict or enhance the possibilities of her political participation? One of the best-founded assertions of political participation literature is that one's work is related to one's political activism. Since the American work force is not integrated by gender, it may be that woman's work limits her political activism. The first major issue, considered in Chapter III, is the extent to which women's work is related to women's political participation.

Second, to what extent does a woman's location in a particular political generation affect her political activism? Women in the United States were not enfranchised until 1920, and feminist movements have appeared cyclically throughout American history. To what extent does exposure to or membership in a ''feminist'' political generation encourage women's political participation? Likewise, does the absence of a nationwide feminist movement make a difference to other kinds of political participation among the mass of American women? Chapter IV will examine how women's membership in a particular political generation is related to political participation.

Third, to what extent is women's political participation affected by feminism? It is, after all, the resurgence of the feminist movement in the United States that has made women's political participation a salient issue once again. There is already a developing literature on feminism and women's voting behavior.[26] Chapter V focuses on the relationship between feminism and additional forms of political participation.

These three explanations of women's political participation can be constructed as three different models: a ''woman's work'' model, a ''woman's political history'' model, and a ''feminism'' model. An investigation of each of these explanations serves as the basis for the following chapters. The concluding chapters will consider the extent to which these explanations compete with or complement each other, will investigate the impacts of race and class upon women's participation, will summarize the changes in women's political participation during the past quarter century, and will evaluate the importance of these changes for understanding American political participation in general. As a prelude to presenting, testing, and comparing these three explanations, Chapter II presents the bivariate relationships between gender and participation.

IS IT POSSIBLE TO RESOLVE QUESTIONS OF WOMEN'S POLITICAL PARTICIPATION WITH AVAILABLE MASS SURVEY DATA?

Since the purpose of this study is to examine women's political participation over time, the most useful set of data on which to rely is the University of Michigan's Inter-University Consortium for Political and Social Research (ICPSR) American National Election Studies. These provide the scholar with roughly comparable sets of data for large, nationally representative samples from 1948 to the present. By relying on the data available for presidential election years from 1952 to 1976, the possibility of electoral participation is maximized, since such elections generate more political interest, involvement, and participation than do off-year elections—or years in which elections are not held.[27] The ICPSR data are especially appropriate for longitudinal study, since the same or similar questions about participation reappear in each study after 1952.[28]

While the ICPSR data are appropriate for longitudinal purposes, they are not as useful as they might be for studying women's political participation; and even for the most recent sample years there are few questions, if any, about nonelectoral community participation. Despite the riots and mass demonstrations in the United States in the late 1960s and early 1970s, it is not until the 1976 study that there are questions about protest activism. There are also some "personal background" and demographic variables that would be useful for the study of women's political participation that are missing. For 1952 and 1972, for example, there are no data available concerning the age and number of the respondent's children. It is not until the 1976 survey that questions concerning the respondent's individual income—independent of family income—are asked; such information would allow us to investigate the differences in participation among women with their own income (independent of their spouse's) and those women who are economically dependent upon the income of a husband.[29] Despite these lacunae in the ICPSR studies, however, they still remain a useful source of longitudinal study of women's political participation.[30]

There are several distinct forms of participation which can be examined using the ICPSR data. These include voting, electoral activism, conventional participation, nonelectoral unconventional activism, political involvement, and political efficacy. *Voting* and *electoral activism* need little explanation or defense as measures of political participation.[31] *Conventional nonelectoral participation* includes those activities which are not centered on election campaigns and which, for the most part, originate with the individual.[32] These might include writing letters to government officials, school board activism, organizing around a community problem, or involvement in community or neighborhood groups. *Unconventional activities* are also independent of elections but are those considered outside of "normal" political discourse, such as demonstrations, protest activities, or civil disobedience. *Political involvement* is included as a participation variable in an attempt, limited by the data, to broaden the definition to include women who, because of material or social restrictions, find it difficult to engage in politics directly, but who nevertheless feel connected to and interested in political discourse. Political involvement encompasses attentiveness to politics and exposure to the media. Finally, *political efficacy*—that is, the feeling that government and politics are comprehensible to the average person—is included, since it may be that political inefficacy is a major barrier to women's participation, while a minor barrier for men.

These categorizations of political participation make sense conceptually; and a correlation matrix of these variables shows that each type of political activity is, in fact, distinct from its counterparts. For a full description of the indices constructed to measure electoral, conventional and unconventional activity, and political involvement, see Chapter II, to which we now turn.

NOTES

1. Some examples of studies of female elites in the United States are: Irene Diamond, *Sex Roles in the State House* (New Haven: Yale University Press, 1977); Janet A. Flammang, ed., *Political Women: Current Roles in State and Local Government* (Beverly Hills, Calif.: Sage, 1984); Marianne Githens and Jewel L. Prestage, eds., *A Portrait of Marginality: The Political Behavior of the American Woman* (New York: David McKay, 1977), Chapters 7 through 14, 16, 17, 18, and 23; Jeane J. Kirkpatrick, *Political Woman* (New York: Basic Books, 1974), and *The New Presidential Elite* (New York: Russell Sage, 1976), Part II; Marcia Manning Lee, "Why Few Women Hold Public Office: Democracy and Sex Roles," *Political Science Quarterly*, XCI (2), Summer 1976, pp. 297–314; Ruth B. Mandel, *In the Running: The New Woman Candidate* (New Haven: Ticknor and Fields, 1981); and Vicky Ran-

dall, *Women and Politics* (New York: St. Martin's Press, 1982), Chapter 3.

2. See Angus Campbell, et al., *The American Voter* (New York: Wiley, 1960), p. 484, where a 10 percent difference ("an over-all estimate") in turnout in the 1960 presidential election was found (the actual male-female difference in turnout for 1960 is 9.1 percent); this "10 percent difference" is cited by many scholars; for example, see Lester Milbrath and M. L. Goel, *Political Participation* (Chicago: Rand McNally, 1977), p. 117. See also Ethel Klein, *Gender Politics* (Cambridge, Mass.: Harvard University Press, 1984), p. 143, where she writes: "As late as 1960, women's participation rate was 11 percent below that of men."

3. Berenice A. Carroll, "Review Essay: Political Science, Part I: American Politics and Political Behavior," *Signs*, V (2), 1979, p. 292 and p. 299. See also Judith Evans, "Women and Politics: A Re-Appraisal," *Political Studies*, XXVIII (2), June 1980, pp. 210–221.

4. Susan Bourque and Jean Grossholtz, "Politics as Unnatural Practice: Political Science Looks at Female Participation," *Politics and Society*, IV (2), Winter 1974, p. 263.

5. See Bourque and Grossholtz, "Politics as Unnatural Practice."

6. There has been renewed interest in the voting choices of American women, as a result of the gender gap evidenced in the results of the 1980 presidential election; see, for examples, Klein, *Gender Politics*, Chapter Nine and the Conclusion. Klein claims that a "feminist vote" had developed as early as 1972 and that a "women's vote" made a difference in the outcome of the 1976 presidential election. See also Sandra Baxter and Marjorie Lansing, *Women and Politics* (Ann Arbor: University of Michigan Press, 1983), Chapter Two, where they claim, "The increasing tendency for women to vote during elections and engage in other political activities at the same rates as men is producing a women's vote margin of growing size and political importance." (p. 24).

For an excellent analysis of women's voting as political strategy, see Mary Fainsod Katzenstein, "Feminism and the Meaning of the Vote," *Signs*, X (1), 1984, pp. 4–26.

7. In this work, I recognize the conventional distinctions among "sex," "gender," and "gender role," where "sex" is the biological fact of being male or female (with recognition that anatomy is occasionally ambiguous), where "gender" is the social identification of one's sex (with recognition that assignment of gender at birth may occasionally be mistaken), and where "gender role" consists of the conglomeration of society's expectations of one's behavior based upon one's gender. Some authors use "sex role" as a synonym for gender role. While Helena Lopata and Barrie Thorne are critical of the use (and utility) of the term "sex role," they write that it "does have the virtue of affirming that one's focus is learned, cultural, and social behavior and not the biological or more narrowly sexual aspects of female and male." See

Helena Z. Lopata and Barrie Thorne, "On the Term 'Sex Roles'," *Signs*, III (3), Spring 1978, p. 720. See also Jessie Bernard, *Women and the Public Interest: An Essay on Policy and Protest* (Chicago: Aldine-Atherton, 1971), pp. 16–24; and Marie Richmond-Abbott, *Masculine and Feminine: Sex Roles over the Life Cycle* (Reading, Mass.: Addison-Wesley, 1983), p.v. I am grateful to Jo-Ellen Asbury for providing me with this last source. In this work, "sex" and "gender" are occasionally used interchangeably, when referring simply to women and men; "gender related" is employed to describe behavior or attitudes which may vary—or are thought to vary—with gender assignment. This usage indicates that I assume the following: first, there is no biological basis for political participation differences between women and men; second, what differences do exist, if any, are socially constructed; and third, that male-female participation differences change over time. See also Virginia Sapiro, *The Political Integration of Women* (Urbana, Ill.: University of Illinois Press, 1983), pp. 57–61; and Wilma Rule Krauss, "Political Implications of Gender Roles: A Review of the Literature," *American Political Science Review*, LXVIII (4), December 1974, p. 1707.

8. Baxter and Lansing, *Women and Politics*, p. 38, emphasis in original.

9. Ibid.

10. Raymond E. Wolfinger and Stephen J. Rosenstone, *Who Votes?* (New Haven: Yale University Press, 1980), pp. 42–43, emphasis in original.

11. See, for example, Klein, *Gender Politics*, p. 122, where she argues that women's support for feminism derives from their personal experiences, primarily in the disjunction between "nontraditional roles" in the labor force and "traditional responsibilities" of being wives and mothers; while "[m]en learn to be feminists vicariously, by evaluating women's claims in terms of abstract commitments to rights, equality, and social justice."

12. See Sidney Verba and Norman Nie, *Participation in America* (New York: Harper and Row, 1972); and Sidney Verba, Norman Nie, and Jae-On Kim, *Participation and Political Equality* (Cambridge: Cambridge University Press, 1978).

13. For a discussion about majority and minority support for feminist issues, and changes in public opinion, see: Baxter and Lansing, *Women and Politics*, pp. 206–209; Janet Boles, *The Politics of the Equal Rights Amendment: Conflict and the Decision Process* (New York: Longman, 1979), pp. 51–56 and 101–103; Zillah Eisenstein, "The Sexual Politics of the New Right: Understanding the 'Crisis of Liberalism' for the 1980s," in Nannerl O. Keohane, Michelle Z. Rosaldo, and Barbara C. Gelpi, eds., *Feminist Theory: A Critique of Ideology* (Chicago: University of Chicago Press, 1982), pp. 77–98; Zillah Eisenstein, "Antifeminism in the Politics and Election of 1980," *Feminist Studies*, VII (2), Summer 1981, pp. 187–205; and Klein, *Gender Politics*, Chapter Six.

14. For a discussion of women's attitudes and vote choices in 1980, see Klein, *Gender Politics*, Chapter Nine; and Baxter and Lansing, *Women and Politics*, Chapter Nine.

15. Carroll, "Review Essay, Part I," p. 303.

16. Temma Kaplan, "Female Consciousness and Collective Action: The Case of Barcelona, 1910–1918," in Keohane et al., *Feminist Theory*, p. 58. I thank Mary Addis for drawing my attention to Kaplan's essay.

17. Nannerl O. Keohane and Barbara C. Gelpi, "Foreward" in Keohane et al., *Feminist Theory*, p. x.

18. Kaplan, "Female Consciousness," p. 61.

19. Ibid., p. 76.

20. Ibid.

21. Berenice A. Carroll, "Review Essay: Political Science, Part II: International Politics, Comparative Politics, and Feminist Radicals," *Signs*, V (3), 1980, p. 459.

22. Baxter and Lansing, *Women and Politics*, p. 221.

23. Michelle Z. Rosaldo, "The Use and Abuse of Anthropology: Reflections on Feminism and Cross-Cultural Understanding," *Signs*, V (3), 1980, p. 417.

24. For writings by feminist theorists on motherhood and its (potential) political implications, see, for examples, Jean Bethke Elshtain, "Feminism, Family, and Community," *Dissent*, Fall 1982, pp. 442–449; and the excellent and highly critical responses by Barbara Ehrenreich and Marshall Berman, *Dissent*, Winter 1983, pp. 103–106, and Spring 1983, pp. 247–249, respectively; Kaplan, "Female Consciousness"; Sara Ruddick, "Maternal Thinking," *Feminist Studies*, VI (2), Summer 1980, pp. 342–367; Mary G. Dietz, "Citizenship with a Feminist Face: The Problem with Maternal Thinking," *Political Theory*, XIII (1), February 1985, pp. 19–37; and Jean Bethke Elshtain, "Reflections on War and Political Discourse: Realm, Just War, and Feminism in a Nuclear Age," *Political Theory*, XIII (1), February 1985, pp. 39–57. See also Judith Stacy, "The New Conservative Feminism," *Feminist Studies*, IX (3), Fall 1983, pp. 559–583, where she characterizes "conservative feminism" (what I would call "reactionary feminism") as one which "affirms gender differentiation and celebrates traditionally feminine qualities, particularly those associated with mothering" (p. 562); and Judith Evans, "The Good Society? Implications of a Greater Participation by Women in Public Life," *Political Studies*, XXXII (4), December 1984, pp. 618–626. Note that empirical studies of political behavior have frequently found that motherhood is an impediment to women's political participation (primarily electoral). For examples, see Campbell et al., *The American Voter*, p. 258; Gabriel Almond and Sidney Verba, *The Civic Culture* (Boston: Little, Brown, 1963), pp. 387–400; Susan Welch, "Women as Political Animals? A Test of Some Explana-

tions for Male-Female Political Participation Differences," *American Journal of Political Science*, XXI (4), November 1977, pp. 714–715. Others have found that motherhood stifles some forms of political participation but enhances others. See Sapiro, *Political Integration*, pp. 134–138; and M. Kent Jennings, "Another Look at the Life Cycle and Political Participation," *American Journal of Political Science*, XXIII (4), November 1979, pp. 755–771.

25. For a discussion of the social construction of women's status, see Rosaldo, "The Use and Abuse of Anthropology," pp. 394–395, where she writes:

Male dominance is evidenced, I believe, when we observe that women almost everywhere have daily responsibilities to feed and care for children, spouse, and kin. . . . Women's goals themselves are shaped by social systems which deny them ready access to the social privilege, authority, and esteem enjoyed by a majority of men.

26. See Baxter and Lansing, *Women and Politics*; Klein, *Gender Politics*; Claire Fulenwider Knoche, *Feminism in American Politics: A Study of Ideological Influence* (New York: Praeger, 1980); and Sapiro, *Political Integration of Women*.

27. For the differences in voter turnout for presidential and congressional elections, see William Crotty, *American Parties in Decline*, 2d ed. (Boston: Little, Brown, 1984), Table I.2, p. 7.

28. For a discussion of the reliability and validity of the ICPSR American National Election Studies, see Baxter and Lansing, *Women and Politics*, pp. 10–12.

29. Eileen L. McDonagh examines the extent to which "achieved" and "derived" status have an impact upon women's political participation. "Achieved" status is determined by the respondent's occupational status (blue-collar, white-collar, and professional/managerial); "derived" status, "applicable only to housewives," incorporates "the occupational prestige of their husband's job." See Eileen L. McDonagh, "To Work or Not to Work: The Differential Impact of Achieved and Derived Status upon the Political Participation of Women, 1956–1976," *American Journal of Political Science*, XXVI (2), May 1982, p. 283. McDonagh's work, in part, gets around the problem of lack of availability of respondent's income data.

30. Most studies of women's political participation which employ survey research data rely on the ICPSR studies; examples are Kristi Andersen, "Working Women and Political Participation, 1952–1972," *American Journal of Political Science*, XIX (3), August 1975, pp. 439–453; Baxter and Lansing, *Women and Politics*; Klein, *Gender Politics*; Knoche, *Feminism in American Politics*; and Welch, "Women as Political Animals?"

31. Voting and electoral activism are treated as separate categories; correlation matrices show little relationship between these two types of partici-

pation (for the years 1952 to 1976). Verba and Nie, *Participation in America*, using cluster analysis, found separate clusters representing groups of citizens whose primary political activity was voting ("voting specialists") and others whose primary political focus was campaign activism, among other kinds of activities.

32. For a discussion of the differences in "individually" and "socially" based conventional nonelectoral participation, see Micheal W. Giles and Marilyn K. Dantico, "Political Participation and Neighborhood Social Context Revisited," *American Journal of Political Science*, XXVI (1), February 1982, pp. 144–150.

CHAPTER II

THE BIVARIATE RELATIONSHIP: GENDER AND POLITICAL BEHAVIOR

The argument that women's political participation is slightly lower than that of men has very little basis of support in ICPSR data. The bivariate relationships between a variety of participation variables and gender show only slight differences, ones that are usually statistically insignificant, not unidirectional, or have been disappearing over the course of time. This chapter presents data on the bivariate relationships between participation and gender, in an attempt to assess the claims of some that gender related differences in participation are dramatic and enduring.

Comparing gender related participation from 1952 to 1976 on several participation indicators, we see a consistent pattern of minor differences in the early 1950s, diminishing in strength and significance and, occasionally, changing direction. Table 1 shows gender related differences for these participation variables: giving money, attending political meetings, working for a political party, belonging to a political organization, attempting to influence the vote of another person, wearing a campaign button or displaying campaign literature, and voting at various levels. Percentage differences are presented: positive values, unless otherwise noted, indicate that being male is associated with higher levels of participation; negative values indicate that being female is associated with higher levels of participation. Significance levels of Chi square are given in parentheses. Phi values are displayed to indicate the strength of relationship between behavior and gender.

In almost none of the types of participation is there a strong or

Table 1.
The Bivariate Relationship between Participation and Gender, 1952–1976

	1952	1956	1960	1964	1968	1972	1976
Gave money to a political campaign	0.09 (.001) 3.8%	0.05 (.03) 2.7%	0.00 * -.03%	0.06 (.03) 3.3%	0.01 * 5.0%	0.05 (.04) 2.8%	0.08 (.001) 4.2%
Attended a political meeting	.02 * 1.2%	.05 (.03) 2.8%	.05 * 2.7%	.04 * 2.1%	.02 * 1.0%	.03 * 1.6%	.02 (.001) -1.1%
Worked for a political party	.05 (.02) 1.8%	.01 * 0.3%	.02 * 1.1%	.01 * 0.5%	.01 * -0.2%	.03 * -1.5%	.00 * -0.1%
Was a member of a political organization	.01 * 0.3%	.04 * 1.2%	.00 * -0.2%	**	.00 * 0.2%	**	**
Attempted to influence another's vote	**	.15 (.001) 13.4%	**	**	.14 (.001) 13.3%	.10 (.001) 9.1%	.13 (.001) 12.7%
Wore a campaign button or displayed campaign literature	**	.08 (.001) 6.0%	.01 * -1.0%	.02 * 1.5%	.03 * 2.4%	.00 * -0.1%	.02 (.001) -1.1%

Presidential vote	.04 * 1.4%	.13 (.001) 11.9%	.11 (.001) 9.1%	.05 (.02) 3.8%	.06 (.03) 5.0%	.07 (.001) 6.3%	.10 (.001) 9.1%
Senate vote	.03 * 1.2%	.08 (.02) 3.6%	.07 * 3.4%	-.01 * -0.3%	.02 * 1.2%	.01 * -0.6%	.07 (.001) 3.1%
House vote	.03 * 1.3%	.07 (.02) 3.7%	.05 * 3.6%	.00 * 0.1%	.02 * 1.1%	.04 * -2.6%	.02 (.002) 1.4%

*p > .05.

**No data available for this question for this year.

Note:
The first figure presented is the phi value, with significance levels (where p is no greater than .05) in parentheses. The third figure is the percentage of active men minus the percentage of active women. All variables have been dichotomized.

significant relationship to gender. In many types of participation, such as working for a political party or voting for offices other than presidential, the relationships between gender and participation have rarely been statistically significant. In only one case—that of attempting to influence the vote of another person—is being male more likely to predict participation; here, the phi value exceeds .10 for most years and is statistically significant at the .001 level. Being male also predicts participation in presidential elections, but the phi values reach the .10 level only in 1956, 1960, and 1976; percentage differences vary as well.

An examination of attitude variables that measure predisposition toward political participation reveals some gender related differences, but these too are slight and again diminish over time. Tables 2 and 3 demonstrate this for the attitude variables: people have no say about government, politics are too complicated, public opinion is unimportant, and voting is the only influence people have. Exposure variables for 1952 to 1976 include newspaper, radio, television, and magazine exposure.

Of the efficacy variables, the only one which demonstrates some gender related difference on its face is "politics is too complicated to understand" (see Table 2).[1] From 1952 to 1976, the percentage differences between women and men are greater than 10 percent, with women more likely than men to agree with the statement. This relationship persists across twenty years and is statistically significant at the .001 level, the phi values indicating the strength of the relationship between gender and support for the statement are consistently greater than .10. We will further examine differences between women and men in feelings of political efficacy in the following chapters, since it is interesting that this difference persists across time but is not reflected in a concomitant difference in reported participation.

The exposure variables demonstrate an interesting characteristic (see Table 3). Women are as likely to rely on radio, television, and magazine exposure for their political information as are men, but they are less likely to rely on newspapers. This difference is reflected in percentage differences greater than ten, significant at the .001 level for most years. However, by 1972 the difference between men's and women's newspaper use has diminished to 5.9 percent, negligible and statistically insignificant. Men are still, in 1976, more likely to rely on newspapers than are women; the difference is 11 percent, statistically

Table 2.
The Bivariate Relationship between Efficacy Variables and Gender, 1952–1976

	1952	1956	1960	1964	1968	1972	1976
People have no say about government	0.08 (.001) -7.4%	0.09 (.001) -8.2%	0.01 * -0.6%	0.03 * -2.9%	0.05 * -4.2%	**	0.01 * 1.1%
Politics is too complicated to understand	.17 (.001) -15.2%	.13 (.001) -13.1%	.13 (.001) -12.9%	.11 (.001) -10.3%	.11 (.001) -10.6%	.13 (.001) -11.8%	.15 (.001) -13.4%
Public opinion is unimportant to elected officials	.04 * -4.3%	.00 * 0.2%	.02 * -1.5%	.01 * 0.5%	.07 .02 -6.2%	**	.03 (.001) -2.9%
Voting is a citizen's only influence in government	.03 * -2.4%	.08 (.001) -7.0%	.05 * -4.8%	.03 * -2.8%	.05 * -4.8%	.003 (.001) -5.8%	.04 (.001) -4.1%

*p > .05.

**No data available for this question for this year.

Note:

The first figure presented is the phi value, with significance levels (where p is no greater than .05) in parentheses. The third figure is the percentage of men agreeing with the statement minus the percentage of women agreeing with the statement. Negative correlation coefficients indicate that being female is predictive of agreement with the statement. All efficacy variables are dichotomous.

Table 3.

The Bivariate Relationship between Media Exposure and Gender, 1952–1976

	1952	1956	1960	1964	1968	1972	1976
Newspaper exposure	0.10 (.001) 8.0%	0.14 (.001) 13.3%	0.09 (.000) 7.9%	0.04 * 3.6%	0.09 (.001) 8.3%	0.06 * 5.9%	0.12 (.001) 11.0%
Radio exposure	.04 * 3.7%	.05 (.04) 5.0%	.05 * 5.0%	.05 * 4.6%	.08 (.005) 7.0%	.08 (.001) 8.5%	.11 (.001) 10.6%
Television exposure	.05 * 5.0%	.04 * 4.0%	.02 * 1.4%	.00 * - 0.4%	.07 (.02) 5.7%	.06 * 3.9%	.05 (.001) 3.3%
Magazine exposure	.03 * 3.3%	.08 (.001) 7.1%	.04 * 3.8%	.04 * 3.3%	.04 * 3.4%	.05 * 4.8%	.08 (.001) 8.5%

*$p > .05$.

Note:

The first figure presented is the phi value, with significance levels (where p is no greater than .05) in parentheses. The third figure is the percentage of active men minus the percentage of active women. Exposure variables have been dichotomized; exposure includes both frequent and occasional media use.

Table 4.
The Bivariate Relationship for Interest and Gender, Various Years

	1952	1956	1960	1964	1968	1972	1976
Pay attention to political campaigns	**	0.09 (.001) 8.0%	**	0.04 * 3.1%	0.05 (.04) 4.2%	**	**
Interest in campaigns	.05 (.03) 4.8%	**	.10 (.001) 8.7%	.04 * 3.4%	.16 (.001) 14.9%	.08 (.001) 7.3%	.03 (.001) 2.5%
General political interest level	**	**	**	**	.16 (.001) 13.9%	.14 (.001) 12.2%	.19 (.001) 5.6%
Follows politics	**	**	.17 (.001) 16.5%	.08 (.001) 5.4%	**	**	**

*p > .05.

**No data available for this question for this year.

Note:

The first figure presented is the phi value, with significance levels (where p is no greater than .05) in parentheses. The third figure is the percentage of politically interested men minus the percentage of politically interested women. All variables have been dichotomized.

Table 5.
The Bivariate Relationship for Information and Gender, Various Years

	1960	1964	1968	1972	1976
Majority party last Congress	0.17 (.001) 16.2%	0.17 (.001) 16.4%	0.06 (.05) 2.5%	0.22 (.001) 21.3%	0.08 (.001) 4.1%
Majority party new Congress	.09 (.001) 9.1%	.16 (.001) 12.8%	.04 * -3.5%	.11 (.001) 11.2%	.03 (.001) -1.2%
Is China a member of the United Nations?	**	.03 * -1.4%	**	**	**
Does China have a democratic government or something else?	**	**	**	.04 * -0.9%	**
Does Cuba have a democratic government or something else?	**	.05 * 1.8%	**	**	**
Length of presidential term	**	**	**	.06 * 3.6%	**

Length of Senate term	**	**	**	.14 (.001) 12.6%	**
Length of House term	**	**	**	.08 (.01) 7.5%	**
General information level[a]	**	**	.16 (.001) 15.1%	.17 (.001) 15.8%	.17 (.001) 15.9%

*p⟩ .05.   **No data available for this question for this year.

[a] As assessed by interviewer.

Note:

The first figure presented is the phi value, with significance levels (where p is no greater than .05) in parentheses. The third figure is the percentage of men's correct answers minus the percentage of women's correct answers. All variables are dichotomous.

significant at .001. In general, however, the relationship between media usage and gender is slight and explicable on some basis other than
gender. The phi values show similar results, although these data are
not as consistent or unidirectional as the percentage differences suggest.

One other area of difference is that of "interest," which is measured in the ICPSR surveys by a variety of questions concerning interest in campaigns, interest in the specific campaign at hand, and a general interest in or "following" of politics. The 1968 data contain several
questions about interest in politics at different levels of government,
ranging from international to local politics. The percentage differences
for interest in international, national, state, and local politics, and for
school board activities, follow respectively, with significance levels in
parentheses:[2] 3.2% (*), 1.8% (*), 0.2% (*), −6.0% (.007), and −3.4%
(*).

As Table 4 demonstrates, men were more likely to report an interest
in politics than were women, but the percentage differences vary considerably across time and across variables. For all variables—"interest
in campaigns," "paying attention to campaigns," and "following
politics"—men are more likely to report interest, although the percentage differences are inconsistent and in some cases are statistically
insignificant. In terms of the strength of the relationship between gender and interest variables, the pattern here is somewhat unclear, with
phi values varying between .04 (for "paying attention," 1964) and
.17 (for "following politics," 1960). The variable "general political
interest" is the subjective assessment of the respondent's general interest in politics by the interviewer. Men were seen as being generally
more politically interested than were women. The percentage differences are relatively high for this variable; the relationship is significant
for all years at .001; and the phi values, while weak, are among the
strongest of those presented in Table 4—which probably tells us more
about the subjective views of the interviewers than about the actual
interest levels of the respondents.

A final predisposition variable is that of information about politics.
Its relationship to gender is also inconsistent (see Table 5). In terms
of the subjective assessment of the respondent's information about politics by the interviewer, men were seen as being more informed about
politics than were women. Objective evaluations about political information may be gleaned partially from questions concerning congres-

sional majorities, whether China is a member of the United Nations (1964), whether China and Cuba are Communist governed, and questions concerning the length of terms of office of president, senator, and representative. These objective indicators do not give a uniform picture. The gender related differences in information about length of terms of office are slight and vary depending upon the office. Women and men are equally likely to know what form of government China has and whether, in 1964, China was a member of the United Nations. There were some differences between women and men in regard to knowing which party held the majority in Congress before and after the election at issue; women were somewhat less likely than men to know in each case. These differences do not diminish over time but rather vary from year to year. Percentage differences, significance levels, and phi values all reflect the inconsistent and volatile relationship between level of political information and gender.

CONCLUSIONS ABOUT THE BIVARIATE RELATIONSHIPS: ATTITUDES, BEHAVIOR, AND GENDER

The few differences in terms of the simple bivariate relationship between gender and political behavior are that in terms of predisposition to politics, women tend to be slightly less interested in and slightly less informed about politics and to feel less politically efficacious, while at the same time they participate about as frequently and in as many ways as do men. This suggests that, for women, there is not the clear relationship between predisposition to politics and political participation that there is for men.[3]

The answer may lie partially with the subjective assessments of the interviewer. The "general information level" and "general political interest level" variables for 1968, 1972, and 1976 are based on the interviewer's estimate of the respondent's political knowledge and interest (see Table 5). It may be that interviewers do not perceive women as being as interested or as informed as men are, even when objectively the case is otherwise. Or it may be that women—and men—are giving the "correct" response; that is, women recognize that politics is a man's world and, although women participate in politics, they know that the approved answer is to say that they are uninvolved or uninterested.[4] A final explanation may be that some women actually do perceive themselves as not being very interested in, or informed about, politics.

The issue becomes more complicated when one considers cross-cultural data from Sidney Verba, Norman Nie, and Jae-On Kim. In their attempt to assess the causes of gender related participation differences, Verba, Nie, and Kim hypothesize that the source may be either women's apathy or inhibitions to women's involvement.[5] In their test of these alternative but not mutually exclusive explanations, they examine the balance between political activism and psychological involvement in politics. They argue that: "An inhibition hypothesis will be supported if we find women to be involved psychologically but not active, even if the disjunction between involvement and activity is due to a social norm against political activity *accepted by women*."[6]

Evidence of apathy, regardless of its sources, would be relatively low levels of both involvement and activism among women. Finally, the authors consider the effectiveness of women in converting their individual or institutional resources into political activism; the authors find that: "It appears that increases in individual or institutional resources increase psychological involvement among women more than they do among men. But women start from such a low level of involvement that they never catch up to the male level of political concern."[7]

The authors find that the differences in overall political activism and political involvement between women and men in the United States are very small. What they do not find in their data, collected in the late 1960s and early 1970s, are low levels of political involvement and efficacy of American women paralleled by similarly low levels of political activism.[8] Again, the major area of gender related difference is not political behavior but rather political attitudes which are usually considered to be related to political behavior. American women report less political efficacy and involvement than do men; on the bivariate level, at least, actual participation differences are few and small.

MEASURING PARTICIPATION USING INDICES

Combinations of variables into political indices may be more useful in comparing women's political participation across a twenty-four-year time span. For the purpose of this study, four participation indices have been constructed, using participation variables from the ICPSR's American National Election Studies from 1952 to 1976. The first index measures *electoral participation*. For the years 1952 to 1976, questions concerning whether or not the respondent attended political meetings, worked for a political party, or gave money to a campaign or candidate were recoded as dichotomous variables and then standardized; the new standardized variables were used to form a simple additive index. A second index was also constructed for the years 1956 to 1976, using the questions in the first index, plus two other questions not asked in the 1952 study: whether the respondent had attempted to influence the vote of another person or had displayed a campaign button or bumper sticker. In comparing the two indices for 1956 to 1976, however, no gender related differences are demonstrated by the second index that are not evident in the first; this is hardly surprising, given the low levels of electoral participation for all respondents, regardless of gender. Therefore, the first index, spanning all years of the study, has been employed throughout.[9]

A second index was constructed that measures *conventional nonelectoral participation*. Conventional nonelectoral participation was originally intended to encompass local-level political participation not associated with an election, such as school board participation or neighborhood-focused activism. However, data for these activities were generally unavailable except for 1976. Therefore, conventional nonelectoral activism is measured simply as nonelectoral political expression. For the years 1964 to 1976, ICPSR data include questions of writing letters to government officials or to the editor of a newspaper; these variables were dichotomized, standardized, and used to form a simple additive index. The term "conventional" is employed to distinguish this activity from "unconventional" participation, such as protest activity. The variables employed in the conventional activities index, for the years 1964 to 1976, are: "Aside from this particular election campaign, here are some other ways people can be involved in politics. Have you ever written a letter to any public officials giving them your opinion about something that should be done?" and "Have you ever written a letter to the editor of a newspaper or magazine giving any political opinions?"[10]

Unconventional political participation is measured in two ways: first, as an index of approval for protest activities, demonstrations, and civil disobedience, and second, as actual participation in petition drives and demonstrations. The first measure is available only for 1968 and 1972, while the second measure is available only for 1976. Despite this paucity of data, and despite the fact that unconventional activities are probably best studied with a sample other than a mass national one, these measures are included to give an indication of what the gender related differences are and what the differences are between groups of women. The unconventional activism index for 1968 and 1972, which is really an attitude index, is based on the questions: "How about taking part in protest meetings or marches that are permitted by the local authorities? Would you approve of taking part, disapprove, or would it depend on the circumstances?"; "How about refusing to obey a law which one thinks is unjust, if the person feels so strongly about it that he is willing to go to jail rather than obey the law? Would you approve of a person doing that, disapprove, or would it depend on the circumstances?"; and "Suppose all other methods have failed and the person decides to try to stop the government from going on about its usual activities with sit-ins, mass meetings, demonstrations, and things like that? Would you approve of that, disapprove, or would it depend on the circumstances?"[11] These variables were dichotomized, standardized, and used to form a simple additive index, with each variable weighted equally. The unconventional participation index for 1976, which measures actual participation, was constructed in the same way; it, however, is based on these two questions: "Have you signed a petition either for or against action by the national government?" and "Have you taken part in a sit-in, demonstration, or protest concerned with a national problem?"[12]

Finally, an index measuring *political involvement* was constructed. This variable is included to encompass "spectator" behavior and to extend the range of participation included. An additive index was created from the following questions, which are available for 1952 to 1976: "Some people don't pay much attention to the political campaigns. How about you, would you say that you have been very much interested, somewhat interested, or not much interested in following the political campaigns this year?"; "Did you read about the campaign in any magazines?"; and "Did you read about the campaign in any newspapers?"[13] The variables were dichotomized, with "very much" and "somewhat" interested combined as the positive response to the interest question. Each variable was standardized, and the political interest variable was given twice the weight of each of the other two variables in the index. This is similar to the "political involvement'' index used by Norman Nie, Sidney Verba, and John R. Petro-cik, in *The Changing American Voter*.[14] Two additional single-vari-able measures are employed in this work: voting participation in presidential elections and political efficacy, as measured by disagree-ment with the statement, ''Sometimes politics and government seem too complicated for a person like me to understand.'' Both variables are available for all sample years under study.

The construction of indices provides certain economies of space and time in comparing groups of women and in comparing groups of women and men, across seven presidential election surveys, and provides measures of a considerable range of political activities—from voting to protest participation. In addition, while it may be that there are few differences between women and men in individual participatory acts, there may be an additive effect, measurable by indices, that reveals considerable differences by gender.

Table 6 shows the bivariate relationships between participation vari-ables and gender, providing percentage differences, significance lev-els, and phi values. Again, there are few differences; what differences do exist are usually statistically insignificant or inconstant. Only for involvement is there a difference between women and men. With the exceptions of the years 1952 and 1964, the relationship between gen-der and involvement is stronger than + .10, significant at .001; how-ever, the percentage differences are not dramatic. Again, gender re-lated differences appear in a political attitude or predisposition, while they do not appear—or are less apparent—in political behavior.

To recapitulate, the apparent political differences between men and women, at least in the bivariate relationship, are primarily attitudinal rather than behavioral. Women and men differ in political involve-ment, in feelings of political efficacy, and, in some cases, in political interest, while similar proportions of both vote, are active in electoral politics, and engage in conventional nonelectoral activities. Given that the actual participation differences are small, and that these data span more than two decades, it is astounding that scholars continued to stress male-female participation differences at the mass level long after contemporary data refuted them.[15] On the bivariate level, the issue of massive, mass-level differences has been resolved. However, this sim-ilarity in gender related participation at the bivariate level may mask a considerable diversity in behavior among different groups of women. Women's political behavior may be quite heterogeneous according to race, class, age, or occupation, variations undetectable in the simple

Table 6.
The Bivariate Relationship for Various Participation Indices and Gender, 1952–1976

	1952	1956	1960	1964	1968	1972	1976
Electoral activism index	0.07 (.005) 4.5%	0.05 (.04) 3.5%	0.01 * 1.1%	0.04 * 2.9%	0.02 * 1.4%	0.05 (.03) 3.6%	0.03 (.001) 2.1%
Conventional nonelectoral activism index	**	**	**	.04 * 0.5%	.06 (.01) 5.9%	.05 * 1.7%	.10 (.001) 6.8%
Unconventional activism index	**	**	**	**	.00[a] * 1.0%	.12[a] (.002) 0.7%	.06[b] (.001) 0.4%
Political involvement index	.08 (.04) 5.5%	.15 (.001) 12.3%	.16 (.001) 12.1%	.07 * 6.2%	.13 (.001) 4.1%	.18 (.001) 15.9%	.12 (.001) 5.2%

*$p > .05$.

**No data available for this question for this year.

[a] Measures support for unconventional activism, rather than actual participation.

[b] Measures actual unconventional participation.

Note:

The first figure represents strength of relationship ($\emptyset$ or V), with significance levels (where p is no greater than .05) in parentheses. The third figure is the percentage of active men minus the percentage of active women. Responses to indexes were recoded as dichotomous variables for the purposes of percentage information only.

bivariate relationship. An alternative possibility, however, is that what motivates women's political participation is different from that which motivates men's; the connection between political involvement or political efficacy and political behavior for men may not exist for women. Indeed, there may be alternative sources for women's political behavior rooted in experiences unique to women. These possibilities will be considered in the following chapters when some of the important variables that define women's lives politically, economically, and socially are examined. The following chapters investigate the impacts of three such conditions or experiences unique and potentially politically important to women—women's work, women's political history, and support for feminism—upon women's political participation. We turn first to a consideration of women's work.

NOTES

1. This question asks for agreement or disagreement with the following statement: "Sometimes politics and government seem so complicated that a person like me can't really understand what's going on."

2. An asterisk denotes $p > .05$.

3. In addition, "If there is little evidence of difference between men and women on certain measures of participation, how does one account for the fact that men dominate political life?" Susan Bourque and Jean Grossholtz, "Politics as Unnatural Practice: Political Science Looks at Female Participation," *Politics and Society*, IV (2), Winter 1974, p. 263.

4. Murray Goot and Elizabeth Reid argue that conventional survey questions may solicit artificially low levels of political interest, participation, and competence from women, if the questions hint that politics is a male arena. In these cases, "the interviewees are more sensitive to what the question asks than are the researchers." Murray Goot and Elizabeth Reid, *Women and Voting Studies* (Beverly Hills: Sage, 1975), p. 6.

5. Sidney Verba, Norman Nie, and Jae-On Kim, *Participation and Political Equality* (Cambridge: Cambridge University Press, 1978), pp. 254–255.

6. Ibid., p. 255; emphasis in original.

7. Ibid., p. 262.

8. John C. Pierce, William P. Avery, and Addison Carey, Jr., found a similar discrepancy between feelings of efficacy and actual participation among black women in New Orleans. While black women were found to participate as much as black men, the authors found that "in each case the women have less confidence in their ability to understand or influence politics. The overall equal participation manifested by the women is not mirrored in equal feelings

as to its effectiveness." John Pierce et al., "Sex Differences in Black Political Beliefs and Behavior," *American Journal of Political Science*, XVII (2), May 1973, p. 427.

9. The variables employed in the electoral participation index are: "During the campaign, did you go to any political meetings, rallies, dinners, or things like that?"; "During the campaign, did you do any other work for one of the parties or candidates?"; and "Did you give any money to a political party or make any other contribution this year?" These are questions 0205, 0206, 0204; 0217, 0218, 0216; 0314, 0315, 0335; 0397, 0398, 0423; 0469, 0470, 0473; 3532, 3533, 3535; for 1952 to 1976, respectively.

10. The variables employed in the conventional activities index are numbered: 0318, 0321; 0425, 0428; 9474, 0475; 3537, 3538; for the years 1964 to 1976, respectively.

11. The unconventional activism index for 1968 and 1972 includes variables numbered 0472, 0474, 0476; and 0275, 0276, 0278, respectively.

12. The unconventional activism index for 1976 includes variables numbered 3049 and 3050.

13. These variables are numbered: 0044, 0176, 0173; 0097, 0200, 0196; 0115, 0194, 0190; 0323, 0282, 0279; 0430, 0299, 0292; 0163, 0456, 0461; 3031, 3602, 3645; for 1952 to 1976, respectively.

14. Norman Nie, Sidney Verba, and John R. Petrocik, *The Changing American Voter* (Cambridge, Mass.: Harvard University Press, 1976), pp. 272–277.

15. See the discussion in Chapter 1. For additional examples, see Fred Greenstein, who writes: "Women are substantially less likely than men to engage in the whole range of activities available to the politically interested citizen." Fred Greenstein, *Children and Politics* (New Haven: Yale University Press, 1965), p. 108. M. Kent Jennings and Norman Thomas claim:

The existence of sex differences in political behavior is one of the most consistently reported findings in empirical studies of political science, voting behavior, and political participation. . . . [T]he American differences are substantial. . . . They manifest themselves in a lower level of feminine activity in voting and other more intense forms of participation. . . . The basic conclusion which one derives from the literature is quite clear: men participate more. . . .

M. Kent Jennings and Norman Thomas, "Men and Women in Party Elites: Social Roles and Political Resources," *Midwest Journal of Political Science*, XII (4), November 1968, pp. 469–471.

CHAPTER III

WOMEN'S WORK AND POLITICAL PARTICIPATION

A strong relationship between type of occupation and political participation is well established in political science literature,[1] yet the particular effects of "women's work" upon participation have not been
fully examined. One of the major differences between women and
men in American society is the work that they do, and it is not unreasonable to expect the differences in "women's work" and "men's
work" to have differing impacts upon women's and men's political
participation. The purpose of this chapter is to investigate the importance of the conditions of women's work to women's political activity.

There are three major components of "women's work": 1) paid
employment outside the home, 2) unpaid employment within the home,
hereafter referred to as housework, and 3) childcare. Women's paid
employment outside the home differs from men's paid employment
because women are concentrated in different occupations, under different working conditions, with different expectations, and with different remuneration. The work entailed in housework, for which women
are responsible in American society, includes the maintenance tasks of
the household, such as cooking, cleaning, purchasing, doing laundry,
washing dishes, and other tasks which allow family members to function in society.[2] Childcare is a form of women's work which entails
providing health care for the child; keeping the child clean, safe, and
clothed; directing the child's day (e.g., seeing that the child gets to
school on time, eats meals, goes to sleep); performing "educative
functions," such as playing with the child, disciplining her, reading

to her; and performing monitoring functions (e.g., supervising the child's activities).

Women's paid employment, childcare, and housework differ considerably from work that men do. There is no job of "househusband" in the United States, no formal role equivalent to that of housewife, where household tasks must be performed every day. The responsibilities of childcare, as described above, belong to the mother rather than the father; men do not have primary responsibility for childcare in the United States. Although housework and childcare are conceptually distinct jobs, they frequently overlap and reinforce each other. Paid employments for women and men also differ; usually women's work in the public sphere reflects or duplicates women's work in the home. However, women's work has never been a "given" in society. Divisions of labor between the sexes have never been fixed but have been changing throughout history. In terms of women's paid employment, there have been some important changes in the postwar period.

WOMEN'S PAID EMPLOYMENT

The numbers of women employed in the labor force in the United States have increased since 1952. The percentage of women working, for all women for selected years, has risen from 33.9 percent in 1950 to 37.8 percent in 1960, to 43.4 percent in 1970, to 45.7 percent in 1974.[3] During the same time period, the percentage of men working, for all men, showed a slight decrease of 8.5 percent. This increase in the percentage of women employed in the labor force has occurred independently of women's marital or parental status. The percentage of single women employed has changed, for the selected years 1950, 1960, 1970 and 1975, from 50.5 percent to 44.1 percent to 53.0 percent to 56.7 percent, respectively.[4] The percentage of married women in the labor force has increased more dramatically for the same selected years: 23.8 percent to 30.5 percent to 40.8 percent to 44.4 percent, respectively. This pattern of change is mirrored as well by women with children, although women with children under six years of age are least likely to be represented in the paid labor force. For married women with children under the age of eighteen, the percentage employed in the paid labor force rose from 18.4 percent in 1950 to 27.6 percent in 1960, to 39.7 percent in 1970, to 44.8 percent in 1975.[5]

In addition, women's labor force participation differs from that of

men in that women are concentrated in a few, poorly paid occupations. This job segregation by gender confounds normal analyses dependent upon standard occupational classification. In 1975, 4,314,000
women and 6,517,000 men were employed as "professional, technical, and kindred workers";[6] however, women are concentrated in the
occupations of "health workers" and "teachers, except college and
university," while men are overrepresented as engineers and engineer-
ing and science technicians. In the category of "sales workers," men
are more likely to be real estate agents and brokers, while women are
more likely to be sales workers or retail sales clerks. Men are underrepresented in every occupation within the category "clerical and kindred
workers," while women are underrepresented in the skilled and unskilled industrial occupations. Within the "service workers" category,
women are more likely to be health service or personal service workers, while men are more likely to be protective service workers—or
bartenders.[7]

These occupational variations by gender result in gender related income differences, although the practice of paying women less for the
same work that men do continues to account for some income differences. The median annual incomes for women, for the selected years
1960, 1970, and 1974, were $3,496, $5,440, and $6,957, respec-
tively, while the median annual incomes for men for those same years
were $5,435, $9,184, and $12,152, respectively.[8] Working women
who are married contribute between 20 and 40 percent of their total
family income. For wives with work experience, the contributions to
total family income, for the years 1960, 1970, and 1974, were 20.2
percent, 26.7 percent, and 26.5 percent, respectively. Working wives'
contributions also vary according to the age of the husband and the
work experience of the wife.[9]

These differences in paid labor force participation between women
and men make comparisons based on mass survey data difficult. First,
"professional and managerial" categories include occupations such as
aeronautical engineer, judge, and physician (which require extensive
professional training, are highly paid, and are dominated by men), and
social worker, registered nurse, and kindergarten teacher (which require less formal education, are less well paid, and are dominated by
women). Hence, standard occupational categories frequently obscure
important differences between women and men. Second, as the first
example suggests, "women's occupations" are not as well paid as

"men's occupations." In occupations where women are overrepresented, salaries are considerably lower than are salaries for the occupations where men predominate.[10] Third, even women who are employed in predominantly "male occupations" are paid less than men are for the same work.[11] The phenomenon of "unequal pay for equal work" complicates occupational comparisons between women and men.

WOMEN'S WORK, EMPLOYMENT STATUS, AND OCCUPATION

The positive impact of employment upon political participation is a result of involvement in the collective activity of work, exposure to other adults, and the placement of the worker in the "public" sphere. Because of the special nature of women's work for wages outside the home and the kinds of occupations in which women are employed, an examination of women's work must include both employment status and occupation.

Employment status is defined as employed for wages outside the home, or "employed," in contrast to unemployment and unpaid labor inside the home, or "housewife." An immediate complication arises with this definition, since most married women who are employed for wages outside the home also do unpaid labor inside the home, i.e., housework. The two are not strictly separable. Nonetheless, the experience of being employed outside the home may still have the impact of increasing women's political participation, as it does for men. Kristi Andersen, for example, has found that women who are employed are more likely to participate, and to have positive feelings about their political efficacy, than are women who are not employed.[12] It is expected that women who are employed outside the home will be more likely to participate in politics than their unemployed counterparts and that the differences between these two groups will increase over time.

Occupation makes a difference in the levels of political activity among the mass public. White-collar or professional workers are more likely to participate in politics than are blue-collar or unskilled workers.[13] Among women, some occupations are expected to encourage political participation more than others, according to the conditions of work (can occupational skills be used to develop political participation skills?), the extent to which the work is "public" (does the employee have the opportunity to interact with others?), and the level of income earned. Professional and managerial occupations are most likely to promote political participation among women, since this category is the most highly paid and the most likely to require skills which can be used in political participation. Clerical and sales jobs are less likely to promote political participation, since these types of work are generally done in isolation, do not involve widespread collective effort, and usually prohibit independent initiative.[14] Women are poorly represented in the skilled and unskilled occupations;[15] given the requirements of physical labor (not necessary to political activism), the inflexibility of work schedules, and the relatively low pay levels, women in these occupations will be unlikely to participate in politics.

Therefore, it is expected that professional and managerial women will be most active politically; clerical and sales and skilled and unskilled employees are expected to participate less in politics. However, it is also expected that differences between women in different occupational categories will decrease over the course of the years under study. Second, women who are not employed outside the home for wages are expected to participate less in politics than women who are employed. The nature of housework as women's work is expected to militate against women's political involvement because it is performed in isolation in the private sphere, it does not develop skills which are useful for political activity, and it is unpaid. The occupational categories examined here are the following: professional and managerial, clerical and sales, skilled labor, unskilled labor, and housework. Farm laborers, students, the retired, and the unemployed are excluded.

THE RELATIONSHIP BETWEEN ACTIVISM AND OCCUPATION FOR WOMEN

An examination of women's political participation across occupational categories shows the following (see Table 7). *In regard to voting behavior*, there are no differences between professionally employed women and female clerical and sales workers. As expected, fewer skilled and unskilled female workers vote than their professionally and clerically employed sisters. While these occupational status differences exist, the impact of employment status is less clear. Housewives, for most years, participate more than skilled and unskilled female workers, at about the same rate as clerical and sales workers,

Table 7.
Percent Activist, and Total Number of, Women by Occupation, 1952–1976

	1952	1956	1960	1964	1968	1972	1976
VOTING[a]							
Professionals	**	84.1% (63)	80.0% (50)	85.9% (64)	85.9% (92)	82.0% (154)	81.9% (204)
Clericals	**	81.3 (107)	83.5 (85)	82.2 (90)	81.9 (127)	79.7 (232)	76.1 (301)
Skilled Workers	**	74.4 (43)	73.5 (34)	78.3 (46)	71.7 (60)	67.3 (107)	45.6 (123)
Unskilled Workers	**	45.6 (68)	65.0 (60)	65.3 (72)	50.8 (85)	60.4 (154)	61.2 (121)
Housewives	**	67.4 (626)	71.1 (294)	74.8 (444)	73.4 (394)	66.8 (609)	65.3 (531)
ELECTORAL ACTIVISM							
Professionals	12.7 (55)	19.0 (63)	37.0 (46)	35.9 (64)	20.9 (86)	20.3 (150)	22.3 (188)
Clericals	10.6 (94)	11.2 (107)	28.2 (78)	19.1 (89)	17.6 (125)	18.0 (219)	16.5 (279)
Skilled Workers	5.5 (55)	11.6 (43)	6.5 (31)	10.9 (46)	11.9 (59)	8.7 (104)	6.0 (91)
Unskilled Workers	8.6 (58)	5.9 (68)	13.0 (54)	8.7 (69)	7.4 (81)	9.6 (146)	6.7 (119)
Housewives	8.1 (566)	13.8 (623)	15.1 (272)	12.3 (439)	16.3 (361)	13.4 (583)	13.1 (504)

CONVENTIONAL ACTIVISM							
Professionals	**	**	**	29.7 (64)	31.0 (87)	40.4 (151)	50.2 (201)
Clericals	**	**	**	21.3 (89)	17.6 (125)	31.6 (218)	29.9 (294)
Skilled Workers	**	**	**	2.2 (46)	8.3 (60)	15.4 (104)	16.5 (112)
Unskilled Workers	**	**	**	11.1 (72)	7.3 (82)	15.6 (147)	14.1 (121)
Housewives	**	**	**	16.5 (443)	18.5 (378)	23.7 (583)	23.6 (530)
UNCONVENTIONAL ACTIVISM[b]							
Professionals	**	**	**	**	24.4 (78)	20.4 (189)	3.2 (249)
Clericals	**	**	**	**	10.2 (108)	15.8 (261)	1.6 (349)
Skilled Workers	**	**	**	**	7.8 (51)	16.2 (123)	0.0 (119)
Unskilled Workers	**	**	**	**	15.2 (66)	17.8 (163)	1.1 (142)
Housewives	**	**	**	**	11.7 (300)	13.6 (668)	0.0 (663)

**No comparable data available for this year.

a Voting levels for 1952 are exaggerated, and hence the data are not included here.

b Measures support for unconventional activism in 1968 and 1972, and actual unconventional participation in 1976.

Table 7 (*continued*)

	1952	1956	1960	1964	1968	1972	1976
INVOLVEMENT							
Professionals	48.1 (54)	25.4 (63)	54.3 (46)	44.3 (61)	30.2 (86)	29.3 (80)	33.3 (204)
Clericals	33.0 (94)	14.0 (107)	47.9 (73)	22.5 (89)	20.5 (122)	18.0 (112)	23.2 (297)
Skilled Workers	13.2 (53)	4.8 (42)	24.1 (29)	6.5 (46)	8.8 (57)	16.0 (50)	20.0 (51)
Unskilled Workers	5.2 (58)	6.0 (67)	24.5 (53)	5.6 (72)	16.0 (81)	18.7 (75)	9.7 (124)
Housewives	20.5 (561)	12.9 (620)	30.3 (267)	23.2 (439)	19.3 (373)	22.3 (296)	32.0 (525)
POLITICAL EFFICACY[c]							
Professionals	35.5 (62)	41.9 (62)	50.0 (50)	44.6 (65)	55.9 (93)	31.6 (187)	33.3 (198)
Clericals	29.8 (104)	40.2 (107)	56.0 (84)	34.0 (94)	57.6 (139)	26.8 (268)	23.2 (293)
Skilled Workers	15.0 (60)	18.6 (43)	17.6 (34)	17.4 (46)	34.8 (66)	10.2 (128)	9.8 (93)
Unskilled Workers	10.9 (64)	18.8 (64)	27.1 (59)	17.3 (75)	46.3 (95)	15.2 (178)	6.4 (125)
Housewives	20.8 (610)	30.0 (616)	33.2 (289)	26.1 (467)	49.8 (434)	18.6 (709)	19.7 (513)

[c] Note that efficacy levels are exaggerated in 1968, due to a change in question format.

and less than professionally employed women. We will see this pattern reflected in other forms of participation as well.

The differences in turnout between professional and clerical working women, and between professional women workers and housewives, have remained fairly constant across time; however, the turnout differences between clerical and skilled female workers have increased while the differences between skilled and unskilled working women have decreased. This suggests a growing white-collar/blue-collar split in turnout from 1956 to 1976.[16]

Electoral activism is measured as an index of three variables: attending political meetings, working for a political campaign or candidate, and contributing money. The pattern for women's electoral activism follows that of voting, with professionally employed women participating most and blue-collar working women (skilled and unskilled workers) participating least. While housewives participate less than white-collar female workers, they are more electorally active than blue-collar working women. Electoral activism among all groups of women is relatively low, compared to women's voting participation. Differences between groups of working women, in electoral participation, reveal a pattern similar to that for voting: differences between white-collar and blue-collar workers increased from 1952 to 1976. However, in contrast to other groups of female workers, professionally employed women increased their electoral activism advantage every year from 1952 to 1964, the rate finally slowing in 1968. In addition, the difference in electoral activism for clerical workers, on the one hand, and skilled workers, on the other, increased dramatically in 1968 (to 21.7 percent), a gap that has closed slightly but has been sustained through 1976. For electoral activism, differences between skilled and unskilled workers, for every year, are negligible.

Similar patterns are evident for women's *conventional political behavior*, which was measured as an index containing variables of writing letters to public officials and to newspapers.[17] Conventional activism declines as one moves down occupational categories, again with the exception of housewives. More housewives are conventionally active than blue-collar working women, but fewer housewives are active in conventional politics in comparison to white-collar working women. Differences between groups of women across time, however, show a pattern somewhat different from turnout and electoral activism. The differences among all groups of women remain fairly stable across time, with professionally employed women the most active and blue-collar women the least active; yet for 1976, the conventional activism advantage held by professionally employed women increases dramatically. While the white-collar/blue-collar split is sustained, a professionally employed women/other women split appears in 1976. By 1976, the difference between professional working women and clerical workers is 20.3 percent; between professionally employed women and housewives, 26.6 percent.

Unconventional political participation is measured as an index of support for protest activities, conscientious objection, and civil disobedience (in 1968 and 1972) and as an index of petition, protest, and sit-in activity for 1976.[18] Women's support for and participation in unconventional activism is strikingly similar across occupational categories. Few women of any occupation approve of unconventional activities (except for professionally employed women in 1972); virtually no women participated in unconventional activities in 1976. Differences in support for unconventional activism, between groups of working women, did not change.

Involvement and political efficacy represent two "inactive" or spectator measures of women's participation. *Involvement* was measured as an index of attentiveness to political campaigns and use of the print media.[19] Feelings of involvement vary across occupational groups, with professionally employed women feeling most involved and blue-collar working women feeling least involved (see Table 7). Housewives are again the exception to this pattern. Percentages of "involved" housewives are smaller than those of white-collar female workers but larger than for blue-collar working women. Differences in political involvement between groups of women show the following pattern. Differences between professionally employed women and clerical working women remain fairly stable, as do those between skilled and unskilled working women. However, the gap in political involvement between female clerical workers and skilled working women begins to close between 1952 and 1976, as does the gap between housewives and their professionally employed sisters. What appears in 1952 to be an impressive advantage in political involvement for professionally employed women vis-à-vis housewives, and for clerical working women vis-à-vis skilled female workers, has disappeared by 1976.

Political efficacy was measured as disagreement with the statement that "sometimes politics and government seem so complicated that a person like me can't really understand what's going on."[20] With few exceptions, the pattern for efficacy is similar to that of involvement. Professional and clerical working women report the highest percentages of efficacy, followed by housewives and blue-collar working women, respectively. More housewives feel efficacious than their skilled and unskilled working sisters, but fewer feel as efficacious as white-collar working women. In terms of differences in political efficacy between groups across time, despite some fluctuations, what differences exist remain stable for comparisons among all groups.

To reiterate, for women, occupation and participation are related, for all occupational categories and for all forms of participation (except unconventional activism). However, the occupational status of housewife does not easily fit into the usual explanations of the relationship between occupation and participation. Lester Milbrath and M. L. Goel suggest criteria for ranking occupations by status which presumably assign housewifery a relatively low status.[21] Skilled and unskilled workers have more opportunity in their workplace to interact with others, to participate in union-organizing or community service drives, and to participate in their places of work in ways which might facilitate political participation.[22] Nonetheless, housewives are consistently more active, involved, and efficacious than are their skilled and unskilled working sisters for every participatory form. This may be the result of a greater degree of diversity among housewives than among other groups of women in terms of education, class background, or other variables. The heterogeneity of housewives as a group would both explain their relatively higher levels of efficacy, involvement, and participation, at the same time that it would undermine the connection between the status of housewife and the hypothesized limitations of housewifery to participation.

Table 8 shows the average level of participation (across all sample years for which data are available) for female white-collar and blue-collar workers and for housewives with different levels of educational attainment. Skilled and unskilled women workers have, because of their small numbers, been grouped as "blue-collar" workers; professionally and clerically employed women have been grouped as "white-collar" workers. It is clear that housewives are the most educationally diverse group of women (as well as the most numerous). Almost all

Table 8.
Average Percentage Active Women, by Education and Occupation

	High-school-Educated Women	College-Educated Women
Voting (1952-1976)		
White-collar	80.9%	89.2%
Blue-collar	71.8%	*
Housewives	74.5%	89.3%
Electoral participation (1952-1976)		
White-collar	15.7%	26.4%
Blue-collar	9.3%	*
Housewives	12.2%	26.7%
Conventional activism (1964-1976)		
White-collar	22.8%	42.6%
Blue-collar	11.5%	*
Housewives	20.5%	35.3%
Political involvement (1952-1976)		
White-collar	24.5%	39.8%
Blue-collar	13.4%	*
Housewives	19.7%	42.0%
Political efficacy (1952-1976)		
White-collar	33.7%	49.0%
Blue-collar	21.4%	*
Housewives	27.6%	49.3%

[a]Percentages are averaged across all years for which data are available; years for which the data are available are indicated in parenthesis. Unconventional activism is not included in this table, since support for such activism can be averaged over only two data years, and actual participation data are available only for 1976.

*N<20.

of the blue-collar working women in the sample have less than a high school education, while white-collar working women report over-whelmingly higher levels of education.

The evidence in Table 8 suggests that the differences among different occupational groups of women are not eradicated when the relationship between occupation and participation is controlled for education. While participation is strikingly similar between college educated white-collar female workers and housewives, participation differences remain related to occupation among those with high school educations. White-collar working women in this educational group are the most active and the most involved, and they feel the most efficacious.[23] Blue-collar working women are the least active, least involved, and least efficacious occupational group. The participation levels of house-wives with high school educations fall roughly midway between those of white-collar and blue-collar working women. While education does eliminate participation differences among women of different occupations, it does so only among the college educated; among the high school educated, participation differences among white-collar working women, housewives, and blue-collar female workers remain.

It may be, however, that the "educational diversity" among house-wives is insufficient to explain the participation differences between them and blue-collar workers. A college education or a white-collar job or the opportunity to remain "only a housewife"[24] may provide possibilities for participation that a high school education, a blue-col-lar job, or the need to work outside the home do not. Most women who work outside the home for wages also have the occupation of "housewife"; that is, they bear the burden of women's "double work."[25] Therefore, the additional burden of being a housewife may depress levels of participation that might otherwise be expected from women employed outside the home in blue-collar jobs. This suggests that being a housewife as well as a wage earner is more burdensome for women in blue-collar jobs than it is for women employed in white-collar positions.[26]

The double burden of women's work inside and outside the home might be examined by looking at the differences between the partici-pation of married and single women, using marriage as a surrogate measure for housework and controlling for occupation. A comparison of participation, controlling for occupation, for married women and married men might also reveal the extent to which housewifery limits women's activism but not men's. However, the numbers are so small when the additional control of marital status is imposed that no conclusions can be drawn. The numbers are especially small in the case of single women.

The other possible explanation for the relatively low levels of participation, involvement, and efficacy among blue-collar working women is that, among these women, class norms about women's political participation may act as a limitation to their political activity. The impact of class and class background upon women's political participation will be discussed in Chapter VI.

CHANGES IN PARTICIPATION AMONG WORKING WOMEN

Table 9 summarizes the data in Table 7, to provide information concerning the change in levels of participation among different groups of working women. Andersen found that among white-collar female workers, the number of participatory acts increased over time, starting in 1960, and that blue-collar working women increased the number of their participatory acts, starting slightly later in 1968. Housewives as well increased the number of their political activities, but at a much slighter rate than their sisters employed outside the home.[27] In contrast, Bruce Campbell and others demonstrate that participation, especially voting participation, has decreased among American citizens in general, since 1960.[28]

While it may be that, as Andersen found, these employed women who are active have increased the numbers of political acts they commit (from 1952 to 1972),[29] it is not the case that differences in percentages of participant women have increased. For turnout, in every case, we see the order of activism confirmed: white-collar women, housewives, and blue-collar women. The differences between white-collar working women and their blue-collar and unemployed sisters are large; and, despite fluctuations, these differences between groups remain stable across the years. The same holds true for electoral activism. Again, white-collar working women are most active; blue-collar working women, the least. There was a modest increase in the electoral participation differences between white-collar and blue-collar working women from 1952 to 1976, as well as a modest increase in the differences between housewives and blue-collar working women.

Table 9.
Percent Active, and Total Number of, Women by Employment Status, 1952–1976 (For White-Collar and Blue-Collar Working Women, and Housewives)

	1952	1956	1960	1964	1968	1972	1976
VOTING[a]							
White-collar	**	82.4 (170)	82.2 (135)	83.8 (154)	83.6 (219)	80.6 (386)	78.6 (504)
Blue-collar	**	56.8 (111)	68.1 (94)	70.4 (118)	64.1 (145)	63.2 (261)	53.3 (244)
Housewives	**	67.4 (626)	71.1 (294)	74.8 (444)	73.4 (394)	66.8 (609)	65.3 (531)
ELECTORAL PARTICIPATION							
White-collar	11.4 (149)	14.1 (170)	31.5 (124)	26.1 (153)	19.0 (211)	23.8 (369)	18.5 (476)
Blue-collar	7.1 (113)	8.1 (111)	10.6 (85)	9.6 (115)	9.3 (140)	9.2 (250)	6.2 (210)
Housewives	8.1 (566)	13.8 (623)	15.1 (272)	12.3 (439)	16.3 (361)	13.4 (583)	13.1 (504)
CONVENTIONAL PARTICIPATION							
White-collar	**	**	**	24.8 (153)	23.1 (212)	40.4 (369)	38.2 (495)
Blue-collar	**	**	**	7.6 (118)	7.7 (142)	15.5 (251)	20.0 (175)
Housewives	**	**	**	16.5 (443)	18.5 (378)	23.7 (583)	23.6 (530)
UNCONVENTIONAL ACTIVISM[b]							
White-collar	**	**	**	**	16.1 (186)	18.6 (450)	2.0 (698)
Blue-collar	**	**	**	**	12.0 (117)	17.1 (286)	1.0 (218)
Housewives	**	**	**	**	11.7 (300)	13.6 (668)	0.0 (663)
POLITICAL INVOLVEMENT							
White-collar	38.5 (148)	18.2 (170)	50.4 (119)	31.3 (150)	24.0 (208)	24.0 (192)	27.3 (501)
Blue-collar	9.0 (111)	5.5 (109)	24.4 (82)	5.9 (118)	13.0 (138)	17.6 (125)	12.6 (175)
Housewives	20.5 (561)	12.9 (620)	30.3 (267)	23.2 (439)	19.3 (373)	22.3 (296)	32.0 (525)
POLITICAL EFFICACY[c]							
White-collar	31.9 (166)	40.8 (169)	53.7 (134)	30.2 (159)	56.9 (232)	29.2 (455)	27.3 (491)
Blue-collar	12.9 (124)	18.7 (107)	23.7 (93)	17.4 (121)	41.6 (161)	13.1 (306)	7.8 (218)
Housewives	20.8 (610)	30.0 (616)	33.2 (289)	16.2 (467)	49.8 (434)	18.6 (709)	13.7 (513)

[a]Voting levels in 1952 are exaggerated, and hence are not included here.

[b]Unconventional activism variable represents support for such participation in 1968 and 1972, and actual unconventional participation in 1976.

[c]A change in question-wording in 1968 exaggerates efficacious responses.

**No data available for this year

Differences between white-collar working women and housewives remained fairly constant.

White-collar working women have a considerable advantage over other women in terms of conventional nonelectoral activism. Not only are they the most activist group for all years under consideration (1964 to 1976), but the difference in their level of activism compared to the others is considerable. This large advantage is sustained across all years, increasing temporarily in 1972 but otherwise remaining fairly stable. There is a slight decrease over time between housewives' conventional nonelectoral activism and that of blue-collar working women and a slight increase over time between the conventional nonelectoral activism of professionally employed women and that of housewives (again, see Table 9).

The pattern for unconventional activism—whether its approval or actual engagement—is completely different, in fact, nonexistent. There are virtually no differences between women, regardless of employment status or occupational status; this lack of difference is sustained in 1968, 1972, and 1976—the years for which data are available.

For political involvement, the pattern is again confirmed. Higher rates of political involvement are evident for white-collar working women than for housewives and blue-collar working women; housewives have a higher rate of political involvement than do blue-collar working women. These differences obtain across time, with the exception that the magnitude of the differences between white-collar working women's and housewives' political involvement declines, so that by the 1970s, the differences that exist are minimal.

In regard to feelings of political efficacy, again the pattern is confirmed. More white-collar working women feel efficacious than either housewives or blue-collar working women; blue-collar working women as a group express fewest feelings of political efficacy. The gap in political efficacy, however, between white-collar women and the others is large, and the differences remain stable across time. The advantage that white-collar working women have in terms of political efficacy in 1952 endures through 1976.

Differences in participation levels between groups of women—regardless of employment status or occupational status—have remained fairly stable across time. For all forms of participation, there is an advantage for employed women in white-collar positions. This advantage, again evident in all forms of participation, remains constant across time, with few exceptions. For only one type of participation have white-collar women increased their participatory advantage vis-à-vis other groups of women, and that is conventional nonelectoral activism.

GENDER RELATED DIFFERENCES IN PARTICIPATION BY OCCUPATIONAL STATUS

The participation pattern across occupational categories for men is similar to that for women: professionally employed men are most active, and blue-collar working men are least active politically, for all forms of participation under consideration.[30] As Table 10 demonstrates, however, a simple control for occupation does not eliminate gender related differences in participation; if anything, participation differences seem more evident. Except for support for unconventional participation and actual unconventional activity, men are more politically active than women, independent of occupational category (housewives are excluded). For all years, men are at least 5 percent more participant than women in the following categories. For voting, men are more active than women in sixteen of twenty-eight cases (57.1 percent); for electoral activism, men are more active in eleven of twenty-eight cases (39.3 percent); men are more conventionally active in ten of sixteen instances (62.5 percent); and men are more politically involved in seventeen of twenty-eight cases (60.7 percent). The largest gender related differences remain for political efficacy. Men are at least 5 percent more efficacious than their female counterparts in twenty-seven of the twenty-eight cases under consideration (96.4 percent). They are at least 10 percent more efficacious in twenty-two of those same cases (or 78.6 percent). The fewest gender related differences in participation occur for professionals; the largest number of gender related participation differences occur among clerical and unskilled workers. Still, in one-third of all cases, professionally employed men are at least 5 percent more active than their female counterparts. And, for political efficacy, more male professionals (by at least 10 percent) report feeling efficacious than their sisters for every year except 1964.

Gender related differences in political participation do not disappear when the relationship is controlled for occupation. If anything, because of the large numbers of housewives and their relatively lower levels of participation, gender related differences become more evi-

Table 10.
Percent Active, and Total Number of, Women and Men, by Occupation, 1952–1976

	1952		1956		1960		1964		1968		1972		1976	
	Women	Men	Women	Men	Women	Men	Women	Men	Women	Men	Women	Men	Women	Men
VOTING[a]														
Professionals	*	*	84.1% (63)	89.9% (187)	80.0% (50)	91.7% (120)	85.9% (64)	86.4% (169)	85.9% (92)	88.3% (180)	82.0% (154)	87.5% (282)	81.9% (204)	87.7% (301)
Clericals	*	*	81.3 (107)	86.2 (65)	83.5 (85)	93.9 (49)	82.2 (90)	91.5 (71)	81.9 (127)	91.4 (58)	79.7 (232)	87.2 (121)	76.1 (301)	84.3 (89)
Skilled workers	*	*	74.4 (43)	76.4 (258)	73.5 (34)	79.7 (177)	78.3 (46)	77.4 (212)	71.7 (60)	71.1 (239)	67.3 (107)	73.2 (377)	45.6 (123)	70.5 (237)
Unskilled workers	*	*	45.6 (68)	65.1 (43)	65.0 (60)	77.1 (48)	65.3 (72)	63.9 (61)	58.8 (85)	76.3 (38)	60.4 (154)	65.9 (85)	61.2 (121)	67.5 (191)
Housewives	*	*	67.4 (626)	*	71.1 (294)	*	74.8 (444)	*	73.4 (394)	*	66.8 (609)	*	65.3 (531)	*
ELECTORAL ACTIVISM														
Professionals	12.7 (55)	28.0 (157)	19.0 (63)	23.7 (186)	37.0 (46)	27.0 (115)	35.9 (64)	27.1 (166)	20.9 (86)	22.4 (165)	20.3 (150)	25.6 (280)	22.3 (188)	27.5 (265)
Clericals	10.6 (94)	17.9 (67)	11.2 (107)	21.5 (65)	28.2 (78)	14.6 (48)	19.1 (89)	28.2 (71)	17.6 (125)	22.6 (53)	18.0 (219)	19.1 (104)	16.5 (279)	15.6 (77)
Skilled workers	5.5 (55)	7.3 (240)	11.6 (43)	12.5 (256)	6.5 (31)	15.1 (166)	10.9 (46)	12.4 (210)	11.9 (59)	13.2 (228)	8.7 (104)	12.4 (363)	6.0 (91)	9.4 (203)
Unskilled workers	8.6 (58)	4.8 (104)	5.9 (68)	18.6 (43)	13.0 (54)	19.6 (46)	8.7 (69)	3.3 (60)	7.4 (81)	16.2 (37)	9.6 (146)	12.0 (83)	6.7 (119)	11.8 (186)
Housewives	8.1 (566)	*	13.8 (623)	*	15.1 (272)	*	12.3 (439)	*	16.3 (361)	*	13.4 (583)	*	13.1 (504)	*

[a] Voting levels for 1952 are exaggerated, and hence are not included here.

*No data are available for this variable for this year.

	1952		1956		1960		1964		1968		1972		1976	
	Women	Men	Women	Men	Women	Men	Women	Men	Women	Men	Women	Men	Women	Men
CONVENTIONAL ACTIVISM														
Professionals	*	*	*	*	*	*	29.7% (64)	32.5% (169)	31.0% (87)	33.1% (169)	40.4% (151)	44.0% (291)	50.2% (201)	50.7% (300)
Clericals	*	*	*	*	*	*	21.3 (89)	31.0 (71)	17.6 (125)	36.8 (57)	31.6 (218)	36.9 (93)	29.9 (294)	38.5 (88)
Skilled workers	*	*	*	*	*	*	2.2 (46)	10.9 (211)	8.3 (60)	19.2 (229)	15.4 (104)	22.0 (364)	16.5 (112)	23.7 (236)
Unskilled workers	*	*	*	*	*	*	11.1 (72)	6.6 (61)	7.3 (82)	15.4 (39)	15.6 (147)	20.5 (83)	14.1 (121)	26.3 (190)
Housewives	*	*	*	*	*	*	16.5 (443)	*	18.5 (378)	*	23.7 (583)	*	23.6 (530)	*
UNCONVENTIONAL ACTIVISM[b]														
Professionals	*	*	*	*	*	*	*	*	24.4 (78)	20.8 (159)	20.4 (189)	21.0 (361)	3.2 (249)	2.8 (337)
Clericals	*	*	*	*	*	*	*	*	10.2 (100)	7.5 (53)	15.8 (261)	17.1 (96)	1.6 (349)	2.7 (113)
Skilled workers	*	*	*	*	*	*	*	*	7.8 (51)	9.4 (202)	16.2 (123)	17.1 (443)	0.0 (119)	0.0 (301)
Unskilled workers	*	*	*	*	*	*	*	*	15.2 (66)	12.5 (32)	17.8 (163)	21.4 (98)	1.1 (142)	2.2 (241)
Housewives	*	*	*	*	*	*	*	*	11.7 (300)	*	13.6 (668)	*	0.0 (663)	*

*No data available for this variable for this year.

[b]Unconventional activism measures support for such participation in 1968 and 1972, and actual unconventional behavior in 1976.

Table 10 (continued)

	1952 Women	1952 Men	1956 Women	1956 Men	1960 Women	1960 Men	1964 Women	1964 Men	1968 Women	1968 Men	1972 Women	1972 Men	1976 Women	1976 Men
POLITICAL INVOLVEMENT														
Professionals	48.1% (54)	49.3% (152)	25.4% (63)	27.2% (184)	54.3% (46)	43.6% (110)	44.3% (61)	39.5% (167)	30.2% (86)	39.6% (164)	29.3% (80)	39.2% (152)	33.3% (204)	41.3% (300)
Clericals	33.0 (94)	40.3 (67)	14.0 (107)	22.2 (63)	47.9 (73)	56.5 (46)	22.5 (89)	36.6 (71)	20.5 (122)	32.1 (56)	18.0 (112)	30.1 (46)	23.2 (297)	30.0 (90)
Skilled workers	13.2 (53)	17.9 (234)	4.8 (42)	12.9 (256)	24.1 (29)	39.3 (163)	6.5 (46)	17.7 (209)	8.8 (57)	10.4 (230)	16.0 (50)	20.0 (180)	20.0 (51)	18.5 (238)
Unskilled workers	5.2 (58)	16.5 (163)	6.0 (67)	9.5 (42)	24.5 (53)	45.0 (40)	5.6 (72)	13.3 (60)	16.0 (81)	21.1 (38)	18.7 (75)	31.0 (42)	9.7 (124)	15.3 (183)
Housewives	20.5 (561)	*	12.9 (620)	*	30.3 (267)	*	23.2 (439)	*	19.3 (373)	*	22.3 (296)	*	32.0 (525)	*
POLITICAL EFFICACY[c]														
Professionals	35.5% (62)	55.1% (178)	41.9% (62)	64.5% (186)	50.0% (50)	64.2% (210)	44.6% (65)	52.5% (179)	55.9% (93)	74.0% (200)	31.6% (187)	52.4% (363)	33.3% (198)	55.6% (297)
Clericals	29.8 (104)	44.0 (75)	40.2 (107)	46.9 (64)	56.0 (84)	63.3 (49)	34.0 (94)	55.4 (74)	57.6 (139)	77.6 (67)	26.8 (268)	47.6 (103)	23.2 (293)	41.1 (90)
Skilled workers	15.0 (60)	32.3 (257)	18.6 (43)	39.8 (256)	17.6 (34)	45.9 (172)	17.4 (46)	32.5 (228)	34.8 (66)	49.2 (256)	10.2 (128)	21.9 (452)	9.8 (93)	28.1 (235)
Unskilled workers	10.9 (64)	28.7 (115)	18.8 (64)	58.1 (43)	27.1 (59)	39.6 (48)	17.3 (75)	15.5 (71)	46.3 (95)	54.3 (46)	15.2 (178)	21.7 (106)	6.4 (125)	19.4 (191)
Housewives	20.8 (610)	*	30.0 (616)	*	33.2 (289)	*	26.1 (467)	*	49.8 (434)	*	18.6 (709)	*	19.7 (513)	*

*No data are available for this variable for this year.

[c]Efficacy levels are exaggerated in 1968, due to a change in question-wording.

Table 11.
The Uncontrolled Relationship between Occupation and Participation, Selected by Gender, 1952–1976

	1952		1956		1960		1964		1968		1972		1976	
	Women	Men	Women	Men	Women	Men	Women	Men	Women	Men	Women	Men	Women	Men
VOTING	.05	.10[a]	.10[b]	.17[c]	.13[c]	.17[b]	.08	.17[c]	.08	.15[b]	.18[c]	.12[a]	.08	.22[c]
ELECTORAL ACTIVISM	.02	.26[c]	.10[a]	.10[a]	.19[c]	.05	.17[c]	.23[c]	.05	.17[b]	.15[c]	.14[b]	.09[a]	.14[b]
CONVENTIONAL ACTIVISM	*	*	*	*	*	*	.06	.23[c]	-.03	.14[b]	.22[c]	.18[b]	.17[c]	.19[c]
UNCONVENTIONAL ACTIVISM[d]	*	*	*	*	*	*	*	*	.12[a]	.14[a]	.13[c]	.01	.22[c]	.02
POLITICAL INVOLVEMENT	.13[c]	.37[c]	.06	.22[c]	.18[c]	.22[c]	.11[a]	.28[c]	.05	.35[c]	.13[b]	.23[c]	.05	.35[c]
POLITICAL EFFICACY	-.11[b]	-.20[c]	-.05	-.15[c]	-.17[c]	-.16[b]	-.10[a]	-.26[c]	.01	-.16[b]	-.12[b]	-.13[b]	-.13[b]	-.29[c]

*No data are available for these variables for these years.

[a] $p < .05$.   [b] $p < .01$.   [c] $p < .001$.

[d] Unconventional activism is measured as support for such activism in 1968 and 1972, and as actual participation in 1976.

Note:
   Standardized regression coefficients, with levels of significance, are presented for the bivariate relationship. Positive correlations indicate a positive relationship between occupational status and participation, except for the case of political efficacy, where negative correlations indicate a positive relationship.

dent. Not only do these differences persist, but occupational status predicts male participation better than it predicts female participation. Table 11 shows the uncontrolled relationship between occupation and participation, selected by gender. Figures presented in this table are standardized regression coefficients; positive values indicate that occupational status and political participation are positively related. The relationship between occupational status and participation is stronger for men than it is for women, with few exceptions. Occupation is more strongly related to voting, political involvement, and feelings of political efficacy for men than for women. In most cases, occupation is more strongly related to electoral activism for men than it is for women; the exceptions are 1956, 1960, and 1972. Occupation is more strongly related to conventional activism for men in 1964 and 1968, but differences between women and men disappear in 1972 and 1976. Only for unconventional activism in 1976 and approval of such activism in 1972 is occupation more strongly related to women's participation than it is to men's. However, in only a few cases[31] does occupational status itself contribute more than 3 percent in explaining participation for either gender, once the relationship between occupational status and participation is controlled for class, race, education, and marital status.

The other issue which arises with the examination of occupation and participation for women and men is, of course, that broad occupational categories not only obscure the specific occupational differences between women and men, but they do not address the serious question of income differences between the sexes within those broad categories or even within the same occupation. Again, ICPSR data are not ideal. There is no personal income variable that is independent of family or head of household income until the 1976 survey. The 1976 data are instructive for that year, however, and inspire regret that longitudinal data are not available to permit comparison. Personal income is more strongly related to women's political participation than it is to men's for every political activity examined, and it is more strongly related to women's participation than is occupation (see Table 12). The strongest relationships are those between personal income and electoral activism, involvement, conventional participation, and political efficacy. It is for these same forms of participation that gender related differences in the relationship between income and participation are greatest.

Table 12.
Participation and Personal Income, Selected by Gender, 1976

	Women	Men
Voting	.18*	.14*
Electoral participation	.27*	.15*
Conventional activism	.27*	.13*
Unconventional activism	.09*	.06*
Political involvement	.29*	.20*
Political efficacy	.27*	.13*

*Standardized regression coefficient, p<.001.

The lack of personal income information for the years 1952 to 1972 constitutes a major and serious lacuna. Many of the major problems in comparing occupational status for women and men concern inequalities in income—differences in wages despite similarity of work, differences in actual work despite similar occupational classification—which have been discussed earlier in this chapter. Personal income information permits, in part, an unmasking of gender related differences in employment obscured by standard occupational categorization.[32]

WOMEN'S WORK: CHILDCARE

An important component of "women's work" is childcare. In the United States, as elsewhere, society places "almost total responsibility for the rearing of children"[33] upon women. By the time the average American mother is thirty-four years old, all her children are in school for the major part of the day.[34] Until then, the work of caring for young children defines the mother's day; while it does not require her *complete* attention, this work does require her *constant* attention. It requires "enough of the [woman's full attention] so that she cannot do anything else."[35] The impact of the work of childcare upon public activity is not difficult to understand. "The child severely restricts the woman's mobility. Isolated in her own home in suburbia, she spends most of her time with people under six years old. She is progressively cut off from participation in the world outside the home." [36]

While these comments are descriptive only of unemployed middle-class women, the impact for all women who have primary child-rearing responsibilities is that of isolating mothers from other adults and from public activities, or, if the mother is employed outside the home, of taking up the time after work that fathers are more likely to have for leisure, if not political, activities.

It is not children *per se* that are related to women's political participation, but rather how children are a defining element of women's work. [37] Children who are in school most of the day do not require the supervision of their mothers; children who are grown are no longer "work" for their mothers. It is likely that women with children at home (children under the age of eighteen) will be less likely to participate politically than women without children at home. As children age, the nature of this component of women's work changes. Mothers of children under school age should be least likely to participate in politics at any level, compared to women who have no children at home. A progressive increase in women's political participation is expected across groups of women who have children as the age of the youngest child increases. Finally, women with school-age children, while less likely to participate in politics than women with no children at home, are expected to participate more in conventional, nonelectoral forms of participation.

There may be some reason to believe that for the most recent years women whose children are grown will show an increase in the level of their political participation. Jessie Bernard suggests:

Sooner or later sons and daughters marry or leave home to find their own way. . . . The responsibilities retained by women in this stage of late motherhood for their grown sons and daughters may be greatly attenuated. As startling as anything else in the recent history of women is the phenomenal increase in the labor force participation of women whom the tactful labor researchers label "mature." In 1970, more than half—54.0 percent—of all women between the ages of 45 and 54 were in the labor force—proportionately as many as of women aged 20 to 24. . . . It is hard to think of these women as the harassed and harassing, depressed and depressing interfering mothers-in-law of the stereotypes. [38]

When the work of childcare is completely over for a woman, the chances are that she will be more likely to become politically active than those women who are still working as primary childcarers.[39]

It is expected, therefore, that the more children for whom a mother must care, the less she will participate in politics. Women with no children are expected to be most active politically and women with many children are expected to be least active.

The age of the youngest child may also be an indicator of the specific type of work which a mother must perform. The younger the child, the more difficult and comprehensive the work of childcare. Children over the age of five are usually in school for a large portion of each weekday, and hence the amount of work required to care for grade school children is less than that required for care of preschool children. Finally, children of high school age are able to perform many childcare tasks for themselves, and hence the amount of work involved in caring for high school age children is still less than that required for grade school children. Therefore, it is expected that mothers with very young children will be less active politically than mothers of older children. This seems to be the case for female elite activists. For public officials, "The timing of the decision to run for the legislature was . . . most frequently related to the age of children and the decline of family responsibilities."[40]

Table 13 shows the distribution of political participation by number of children for women and men. The expectation that political participation among women would decline across groups of women with increasing numbers of children is not completely supported by the evidence. First, women with no children are not more active, involved, or efficacious than women with children.[41] The pattern among women, regardless of the number of children they have, is more one of similarity than of difference, with one major exception. Women with four or more children generally have the lowest levels of participation, involvement, and efficacy—but not for every form of participation and not for every year.[42]

Apart from this exception, there is not a substantial variation across groups of women for the years 1956 to 1976 (there are no comparable data on the number of children for 1952 and 1972). In addition, differences in participation between groups of women remained unchanged across time.

Second, number of children has a similar impact upon men's partic-

Table 13.
Percent Active, and Total Number of, Women and Men, by Number of Children, 1956–1968, 1976

	1956		1960		1964		1968		1976	
	Women	Men	Women	Men	Women	Men	Women	Men	Women	Men
VOTING										
No children	74.1% (323)	81.6% (289)	75.1% (223)	81.1% (210)	75.5% (284)	81.4% (236)	76.3% (300)	76.2% (243)	61.6% (216)	65.8% (197)
One child	58.7 (91)	81.0 (124)	71.3 (67)	88.4 (61)	74.4 (93)	79.5 (97)	74.2 (89)	75.0 (63)	69.5 (172)	76.4 (122)
Two children	71.1 (138)	77.7 (108)	78.2 (86)	80.5 (70)	78.5 (95)	83.2 (89)	74.3 (81)	75.5 (74)	72.4 (232)	83.0 (190)
Three children	61.9 (52)	76.0 (57)	73.1 (49)	81.0 (47)	79.1 (72)	73.9 (51)	68.4 (54)	96.4 (53)	72.9 (163)	85.7 (126)
Four or more children	52.0 (51)	73.8 (45)	57.6 (38)	83.9 (47)	71.3 (67)	77.4 (41)	68.3 (56)	80.4 (41)	64.3 (169)	81.7 (127)
ELECTORAL ACTIVISM										
No children	14.0 (61)	15.9 (56)	15.0 (36)	17.4 (47)	13.5 (50)	13.0 (37)	14.9 (55)	19.0 (58)	14.8 (47)	13.5 (36)
One child	12.9 (20)	13.7 (21)	17.2 (15)	16.9 (11)	18.4 (23)	18.3 (22)	19.8 (22)	9.2 (27)	15.8 (37)	11.6 (27)
Two children	13.5 (26)	23.7 (33)	14.6 (25)	25.3 (20)	13.4 (26)	25.2 (27)	12.7 (23)	18.5 (27)	14.1 (42)	18.3 (39)
Three children	8.3 (27)	12.0 (29)	14.1 (29)	15.5 (29)	13.3 (22)	10.8 (23)	20.3 (25)	23.9 (21)	11.9 (25)	21.3 (29)
Four or more children	10.2 (20)	14.8 (29)	23.3 (24)	24.5 (23)	16.1 (25)	22.6 (22)	13.7 (21)	9.8 (25)	10.4 (27)	14.0 (20)

CONVENTIONAL ACTIVISM										
No children	*	*	*	*	*	17.1 (374)	18.3 (289)	16.9 (378)	23.7 (312)	29.6 (347)	29.8 (299)
One child	*	*	*	*	*	17.6 (125)	17.2 (122)	20.2 (114)	14.1 (78)	21.3 (247)	30.8 (159)
Two children	*	*	*	*	*	14.9 (121)	28.0 (107)	19.0 (105)	28.6 (91)	29.6 (314)	36.7 (229)
Three children	*	*	*	*	*	20.9 (91)	18.8 (69)	23.4 (77)	34.6 (52)	30.8 (223)	43.1 (144)
Four or more children	*	*	*	*	*	16.0 (94)	17.0 (53)	12.2 (82)	19.6 (51)	19.7 (261)	28.8 (155)
UNCONVENTIONAL ACTIVISM[a]										
No children	*	*	*	*	*	*		13.7 (307)	12.1 (272)	1.6 (433)	2.9 (361)
One child	*	*	*	*	*	*		11.5 (96)	10.4 (67)	0.0 (281)	0.5 (214)
Two children	*	*	*	*	*	*		11.7 (94)	15.7 (83)	1.5 (366)	0.9 (272)
Three children	*	*	*	*	*	*		14.3 (63)	34.0 (50)	0.9 (264)	0.9 (176)
Four or more children	*	*	*	*	*	*		16.9 (65)	9.1 (44)	0.0 (309)	0.8 (181)

*No data available for this variable for this year.

[a]Unconventional activism is measured as support for such activism in 1968 and 1972, and as actual unconventional participation in 1976.

Table 13 (*continued*)

	1956		1960		1964		1968		1976	
	Women	Men	Women	Men	Women	Men	Women	Men	Women	Men
INVOLVEMENT										
No children	13.9% (432)	17.8% (349)	39.1% (102)	42.7% (236)	22.0% (372)	24.9% (285)	19.7% (371)	26.5% (306)	21.4% (345)	21.5% (298)
One child	9.2 (153)	16.4 (152)	40.7 (86)	38.7 (62)	23.4 (124)	28.1 (121)	21.6 (111)	10.1 (79)	19.8 (246)	25.7 (156)
Two children	15.1 (192)	18.2 (137)	27.0 (99)	43.2 (81)	18.5 (119)	34.9 (106)	19.4 (103)	24.7 (89)	21.9 (318)	28.5 (227)
Three children	18.1 (83)	16.2 (74)	29.2 (63)	39.2 (51)	25.3 (91)	18.8 (69)	17.6 (74)	33.3 (51)	25.2 (221)	29.2 (144)
Four or more children	6.3 (95)	8.2 (61)	28.1 (57)	48.1 (52)	21.7 (92)	20.8 (53)	18.5 (81)	17.6 (51)	15.7 (261)	28.2 (154)
POLITICAL EFFICACY[b]										
No children	31.7 (429)	45.9 (344)	38.6 (293)	46.2 (253)	24.8 (400)	35.3 (312)	48.1 (437)	62.2 (352)	25.7 (335)	35.0 (296)
One child	27.6 (152)	45.1 (153)	35.9 (92)	42.0 (69)	30.0 (130)	42.1 (133)	54.5 (123)	52.6 (95)	22.2 (241)	30.0 (155)
Two children	35.4 (192)	42.3 (137)	31.5 (108)	60.0 (85)	30.7 (127)	42.6 (108)	53.0 (117)	72.6 (106)	23.4 (318)	37.3 (228)
Three children	30.1 (83)	38.7 (75)	36.4 (66)	44.8 (58)	31.6 (95)	37.0 (73)	56.5 (85)	66.7 (60)	22.1 (222)	37.5 (146)
Four or more children	17.9 (95)	32.8 (61)	29.2 (65)	53.6 (56)	24.5 (98)	39.7 (58)	47.3 (91)	51.9 (54)	12.5 (253)	35.5 (151)

[b]Efficacy responses are exaggerated in 1968, due to a change in question-wording.

ipation. Fathers with four or more children at home are also those with the lowest levels of participation among men—but, as for women, not for every form of participation and not for every year. Nor are men with no children substantially more active, involved, and efficacious than men with children. For men as for women, it makes relatively little difference in participation, involvement, or efficacy if one has children; that is, number of children has only a modest influence on participation unless there is a fairly large number of children still at home.

Controlling for number of children at home, however, does not completely eliminate gender related differences in participation. Men are more likely to participate in voting, more likely to be conventionally active (at least for 1968 and 1976), and more likely to report feeling politically efficacious than are women. In the latter case, gender related differences in political efficacy are dramatic and apparently unrelated to number of children at home. Gender related differences are miniscule in regard to electoral activism and to approval of unconventional activism (in 1968) and actual unconventional participation (in 1976). Gender related differences in involvement remain, when men and women with the same number of children are compared, but there is no clear pattern across number of children.

Therefore, while controlling for number of children serves to eliminate some gender related differences in participation, it does not eliminate all—suggesting that number of children has a disproportionately disadvantageous impact upon women's political participation. However, there are few differences among women with differing numbers of children. If childcare limits women's political activism because of the type of work it is, one should see not only differences between men and women but also differences between women with different numbers of children. This second difference is not demonstrated by the data.

First, number of children makes little difference in women's participation until that number of children becomes quite large. Second, the *absence* of children seems to have very little liberating impact upon women's political participation at the mass level. Therefore, an additional factor related to the presence of children and participation among women needs to be considered: the possible confounding impact of the age of the youngest child.

There is only modest evidence that the age of the youngest child (as an important factor in women's work of childcare, when controlled for number of children) is related to a lower level of participation for women than for men. Table 14 shows the percentage differences for women and men where the number of children is two, and where the youngest child is either younger than four-and-a-half years old (preschool) or between the ages of four-and-a-half and fourteen-and-a-half (grade school age). These controls so diminish the number of cases per cell per year that cases have been accumulated across the years 1956 to 1976 (excluding 1952 and 1972, for which no data on children are available).

These data suggest only the following. Among women, the presence of a preschool child (younger than four-and-a-half years old) has a dampening impact upon voting and electoral participation and upon feelings of political efficacy. Mothers of a grade school child (four-and-a-half or older, but younger than fourteen-and-a-half) report slightly higher levels of voting, electoral activism, and political involvement than mothers whose youngest is a preschool child. Only for feelings of political efficacy is the relationship reversed, with mothers of preschool children reporting higher levels of political efficacy than mothers of grade school children.

The relationship for fathers is less clear. Fathers of preschool children are much less likely to vote or to report feelings of political efficacy than are fathers of grade school children. However, the age of the youngest child seems to have no influence—or very slight influence—on fathers' electoral activism or feelings of political involvement. A comparison of mothers' and fathers' political activism according to age of their youngest child shows therefore that the presence of very young children does not have a similar impact upon all kinds of participation, but only upon some. While age of youngest child seems to make the most—and most consistent—differences in the participation of mothers, voting and electoral participation among both groups is most similar, and most similarly affected by, the presence of young children in the home. There is only modest evidence in Table 14 that the younger the child, the more likely the work of caring for that child will limit political participation for women only.

The surprisingly weak relationship between women's work of childcare and political participation does not necessarily lead to a conclusion of no relationship. Given the strong gender related division of labor regarding childcare in the United States, the known relationship

Table 14.
Average Percent Active, and Total Number of, Women and Men, by Age of Youngest Child, Where Number of Children at Home Equals Two, 1956–1968, 1976[a]

	Women	Men
Voting		
Preschool[b]	70.8% (217)	71.7% (181)
Grade school[c]	75.6 (242)	83.2 (239)
Electoral participation		
Preschool	11.7 (215)	15.0 (188)
Grade school	16.2 (231)	16.8 (233)
Political involvement		
Preschool	17.1 (212)	30.9 (171)
Grade school	26.6 (235)	27.6 (229)
Political efficacy		
Preschool	37.2 (220)	32.8 (185)
Grade school	29.0 (243)	40.2 (244)

[a] Due to small numbers, percentages are averaged across the years 1956 to 1968, and 1976. Data on number of children at home are not available for 1952 and 1972.

[b] Children younger than four-and-a-half years old.

[c] Children between the ages of four-and-a-half and fourteen-and-a-half, inclusive.

Table 15.
Participation and Women's Work, by Gender, for Selected Years

	1952 Women	1952 Men	1956 Women	1956 Men	1960 Women	1960 Men	1964 Women	1964 Men	1968 Women	1968 Men	1972 Women	1972 Men	1976 Women	1976 Men
VOTING														
Women's work	*	*	.14^c	.17^c	.15^a	.17^b	.10	.17^b	.09	.19^b	*	*	.18^c	.27^c
Occupation	.05	.10^a	.10^b	.17^c	.13^c	.17^b	.08	.17^c	.08	.15^b	.18^c	.12^a	.08	.22^c
Number of children	*	*	.12^c	.05	.11^a	.04	.05	.01	.05	.12^a	*	*	-.13^b	-.16^c
ELECTORAL ACTIVISM														
Women's work	*	*	.03	.10	.20^c	.05	.19^c	.23^c	.06	.17^b	*	*	.09	.14^a
Occupation	.02	.26^c	.10^a	.10^a	.19^c	.05	.17^c	.23^c	.05	.17^b	.15^c	.14^b	.09^a	.14^b
Number of children	*	*	-.02	.01	.02	-.02	-.06	.04	-.01	-.00	*	*	.01	-.02
CONVENTIONAL ACTIVISM														
Women's work	*	*	*	*	*	*	.11^a	.23^c	.05	.15^a	*	*	.21^c	.21^b
Occupation	*	*	*	*	*	*	.06	.23^c	-.03	.14^b	.22^c	.18^b	.17^c	.19^c
Number of children	*	*	*	*	*	*	.08^a	-.04	.03	-.05	*	*	-.06	-.08

*No data are available for these variables for these years. ^{a}p<.05. ^{b}p<.01. ^{c}p<.001.
Note: Figures are standardized regression coefficients for occupation and number of children, and multiple Rs for "women's work," which includes the joint effects of occupation and number of children. Positive coefficients indicate a positive relationship between the independent and dependent variables.

	1952		1956		1960		1964		1968		1972		1976	
	Women	Men	Women	Men	Women	Men	Women	Men	Women	Men	Women	Men	Women	Men
UNCONVENTIONAL ACTIVISM[d]														
Women's work	*	*	*	*	*	*	*	*	.18[b]	.18[b]	*	*	.10[a]	.05
Occupation	*	*	*	*	*	*	*	*	.12[a]	.14[a]	.13[c]	.01	.22[c]	.02
Number of children	*	*	*	*	*	*	*	*	.09	.13[a]	*	*	.22[c]	-.04
POLITICAL INVOLVEMENT														
Women's work	*	*	.09[a]	.23[c]	.19[c]	.23[c]	.12[a]	.27[c]	.05	.35[c]	*	*	.14[b]	.36[c]
Occupation	.13[c]	.37[c]	.06	.22[c]	.18[c]	.22[c]	.11[a]	.28[c]	.05	.35[c]	.13[b]	.23[c]	.05	.35[c]
Number of children	*	*	.08[a]	.08	.09	.06	-.04	.04	.02	.03	*	*	-.10[a]	-.12[a]
POLITICAL EFFICACY														
Women's work	*	*	.06	.17[c]	.17[b]	.16[a]	.11[a]	.26[c]	.03	.16[a]	*	*	.13[b]	.29[c]
Occupation	-.11[b]	-.20[c]	-.05	-.15[c]	-.17[c]	-.16[b]	-.10[a]	-.26[c]	.01	-.16[b]	-.12[b]	-.13[b]	-.13[b]	-.29[c]
Number of children	*	*	-.04	-.07	-.05	.01	.04	.01	.03	-.02	*	*	-.05	-.01

*No data are available for these variables for these years.

[a] $p < .05$.   [b] $p < .01$.   [c] $p < .001$.

[d] Unconventional participation is measured as support for such activism in 1968 and 1972, and as actual participation in 1976.

Note:

Figures are standardized regression coefficients for occupation and number of children, and multiple Rs for "women's work," which includes the joint effects of occupation and number of children. Positive coefficients indicate a positive relationship between the independent and dependent variables, except for political efficacy, where a negative coefficient indicates a positive relationship.

between being a mother and a woman's political activism at the elite level,[43] the difficulty of using mass survey data to study women's work and participation, and the small numbers of respondents involved, it is more useful to suggest that this link be investigated further, using different data bases, than to conclude that childcare is completely unrelated to women's political participation.

CONCLUSION

The extent to which "women's work" (as measured by occupation and number of children) has an impact upon the political participation of women and men can be seen in Table 15. Standardized regression coefficients are presented to show the strength and direction of the uncontrolled relationships between occupation and participation and between number of children and participation for women and for men; multiple regression values are presented to show the combined impact of the two measures of women's work upon participation, selected by gender. Positive values indicate a positive relationship between the independent and dependent variables, with the exception of political efficacy; here a negative direction indicates a positive relationship between occupation or number of children and feelings of efficacy. Levels of statistical significance are indicated by asterisks.

The data in Table 15 suggest the following. First, there is very little relationship between number of children and political participation, for women or for men, confirming other evidence presented in this chapter. When the relationship is controlled for race, class, education, and marital status, the additional independent contribution of number of children to participation—for women or for men—is less than 3 percent in every case. Again, the lack of evidence for such a relationship for women's mass participation contradicts evidence about the limitations of childcare upon women's elite participation, and hence the conclusion of no relationship at the mass level suggests two things. First, other kinds of data need to be examined; for example, case studies that provide information about the conditions under which women with children engage in or refrain from political participation.[44] Second, it may be that the true limitation of childcare upon women's participation—a limitation which does not operate for men—comes only at the elite level; that is, women's work of childcare may not be particularly politically burdensome to women until they decide to run for elective office or until they consider assuming appointive office.[45]

The relationship between women's occupation and participation is only slightly stronger than the relationship between childcare and participation for women. Occupational status for men seems to be more strongly related to participation than it is for women, with few exceptions, and is statistically more significant than is the case for women. An examination of the joint contribution of occupational status and childcare upon political participation reveals the same outcome: "women's work" explains more about men's participation than it does about women's. However, political participation for both is less related to "women's work" than it is to other variables. When the relationship between women's work and political participation is controlled for race, class, education, and marital status, in only a few cases do occupational status and childcare combined contribute more than an additional 5 percent to the relationship.[46] In most cases, such an additional independent contribution accrues to "passive" types of participation—political involvement and feelings of political efficacy for men.

While "women's work" does not have the unique impact upon women's political participation suggested at the outset of this chapter, it may be that there are other variables of unique importance to women's participation at the mass level. In the following chapter, women's political history as experienced by political generations is evaluated as one such variable. The political history of American women and the experience of political generations of women differ from the political history and experiences of American men. Does a difference in political history explain differences in mass political participation?

NOTES

1. "The more prosperous persons are more likely to participate in politics than the less prosperous." Lester Milbrath and M. L. Goel, *Political Participation* (Chicago: Rand McNally, 1977), p. 96. From the same source, "Persons of higher occupational status are more likely to participate in politics." (p. 102) "Participants come disproportionately from upper-status high education and high income groups. This is clearest if one compares the inactives with the complete activists." Sidney Verba and Norman Nie, *Participation in America: Political Democracy and Social Equality* (New York: Harper and

Row, 1972), p. 100. See Verba and Nie's demographic profiles for various participation types, pp. 98–100.

2. For a discussion of the "emotional maintenance" tasks of housework, see Barbara Sinclair Deckard, *The Women's Movement: Political, Socioeconomic, and Psychological Issues* (New York: Harper and Row, 1975), pp. 59–60; see also Wally Secombe, "The Housewife and Her Labour Under Capitalism," *New Left Review*, 83, January-February, 1973, and Hanna Papanek, "Family Status Production: The 'Work' and 'Non-Work' of Women," *Signs*, IV (4), 1979, pp. 775–781. For a discussion of the amount of time housework requires, see Secombe again, and Joann Vanek, "Time Spent in Housework," *Scientific American*, 231 (5), November 1974.

3. *A Statistical Portrait of Women in the U.S.*, U.S. Department of Commerce, Bureau of the Census (Washington, D.C.: General Printing Office, 1976), Table 7–2, p. 28.

4. Ibid., Table 7–4, p. 30.

5. Ibid., Table 7–5, p. 31.

6. Ibid., Table 8–1, p. 35.

7. Ibid.

8. Ibid., Table 10–1, p. 47.

9. Ibid., Table 10–10, p. 52.

10. Women are disproportionately represented in the clerical work force, for example, while men are found in crafts work in disproportionate numbers. Median weekly earnings of clerical workers in 1979 and 1980 were $195 and $217, respectively, while crafts and kindred workers had median weekly earnings of $305 and $327. Women workers in each of these fields earned considerably less than the median weekly wage. See *Employment and Earnings, January 1981*, U.S. Department of Labor, Bureau of Labor Statistics, Table A–79, p. 83, for these and other depressing statistics.

11. For example, women constituted 78.6 and 77.5 percent of the clerical work force in 1979 and 1980, respectively. The median weekly earnings for female clerical workers for those years were $184 and $204; the median weekly earnings for their male counterparts were $288 and $304. For female professional and technical employees (fields where men predominate), median weekly earnings in 1979 and 1980 were $263 and $289, respectively, compared to male median weekly earnings of $370 and $403. See *Employment and Earnings*, and also *The Earnings Gap Between Women and Men*, U.S. Department of Labor, Office of the Secretary, Women's Bureau (Washington, D.C., 1979).

12. Kristi Andersen, "Working Women and Political Participation, 1952–1972," *American Journal of Political Science*, XIX (3), August 1975, pp. 443–444.

13. Verba and Nie, *Participation in America*, p. 336; Milbrath and Goel, *Political Participation*, p. 104.

14. In assessing the likely impact of type of occupation upon political

participation, one set of criteria is: 1) does the job provide an opportunity (freedom of schedule and blocks of time) for political action; 2) does the job require or develop skills (largely verbal) that can be transferred to politics; 3) is the job sufficiently affected by political decisions that job occupants would feel it important to become active in politics to protect or enhance their positions; 4) does the position become vulnerable if the occupant engages in politics. A second set of criteria is, does the occupation provide: 1) the development and use of social and intellectual skills that might carry over to politics; 2) the opportunity to interact with like-minded others; 3) higher than average stakes in governmental policy; and 4) roles on the job that carry over to public service. See Milbrath and Goel, *Political Participation*, p. 103.

15.   Clerical and sales work occupational categories are dominated by women; the occupational categories of craft and kindred workers, operatives (including transport), and laborers (including farm) are dominated by men. See *Statistical Portrait of Women*, Table 8–1, p. 35.

16.   Differences in participation across time have been calculated from Table 7 for each year and then compared. Differences examined are: rate of participation of professionally employed women minus clerical and sales working women; rate of female clerical and sales workers minus skilled working women; rate of skilled working women minus unskilled working women; and rate of professionally employed women minus housewives. The actual data are not presented in the interests of conserving space but may easily be reconstructed from the data in Table 7.

17.   See Chapter II, fn.10, for an explanation of the construction of this index.

18.   See Chapter II, fn. 11, for a full description of this index.

19.   This index is described in Chapter II, fn.14.

20.   See Chapter II, fn. 1 for a description of the efficacy variable.

21.   See fn.14.

22.   See Carole Pateman, *Participation and Democratic Theory* (Cambridge: Cambridge University Press, 1970), on the workplace as an arena for practicing democracy, especially Chapters III and IV.

23.   The exception is electoral activism, where participation among women of different occupations is very similar.

24.   That is, working only in the home rather than both in the home and outside it.

25.   Using marital status of "married, spouse present" as a surrogate for "housewife," housewives accounted for 55.9 percent of the total female work force aged sixteen and older in December 1980. See *Employment and Earnings*, Table A-29, p. 46 (figures calculated by author from source).

26.   See Eileen McDonagh, "To Work or Not to Work: The Differential Impact of Achieved and Derived Status upon the Political Participation of Women, 1956–1976," *American Journal of Political Science*, XXVI (2), May

1982, pp. 280–297, where she finds that social status derived from one's husband's occupational status may serve as a political resource, especially important for married women who do not work outside the home.

27. Andersen, "Working Women," pp. 442–443. See Figure 2, p. 443.

28. Bruce Campbell, *The American Electorate: Attitudes and Actions* (New York: Holt, Rinehart, and Winston, 1979), pp. 232–236; see Table 12–1, p. 233. See also William J. Crotty, *American Parties in Decline* (Boston: Little, Brown, 1984), Chapter 1, especially Table 1.2, p. 7, and pp. 275–277.

29. Andersen, "Working Women," pp. 442–443.

30. The single exception is unconventional activism.

31. These cases are: voting for men, 1960 (9.7 percent) and 1968 (3.6 percent); voting for women, 1972 (4.5 percent); electoral activism for men, 1952 (7.0 percent) and 1964 (5.5 percent); electoral activism for women, 1960 (6.7 percent); conventional nonelectoral activism for women, 1972 (5.8 percent) and 1976 (6.5 percent); unconventional activism for women, 1976 (6.6 percent); political involvement for men, 1952 (3.8 percent), 1956 (5.1 percent), 1968 (5.0 percent), and 1976 (7.6 percent); political involvement for women, 1952 (26.7 percent), 1960 (3.0 percent); political efficacy for women, 1960 (4.2 percent).

32. However, see again McDonagh,"To Work or Not To Work," for an examination of women's "achieved" and "derived" employment status and its impact upon participation. McDonagh finds that "derived" occupational status, when that status is high, can have an additional positive impact upon the political participation of housewives.

33. Helena Z. Lopata, *Occupation: Housewife* (London: Oxford University Press, 1971), p. 183.

34. Mirra Komarovsky, *Women's Role in Contemporary Society* (New York: Avon, 1972), p. 64, cited in Deckard, *The Women's Movement*, p. 58.

35. Ibid., p. 56.

36. Ibid., p. 54.

37. In fact, "children" can have a positive impact upon women's political participation, at least at the level of local "school politics," an impact stronger for women than for men. See M. Kent Jennings's study based on 1968 data, "Another Look at the Life Cycle and Political Participation," *American Journal of Political Science*, XXIII (4), November 1979, pp. 755–771.

38. Jessie Bernard, *The Future of Motherhood* (New York: Penguin, 1974), p. 193.

39. Again, Jennings's work suggests that this depends upon the *type* of participation one examines. He argues that "the intersection of life-stage properties and the opportunity structure conditions the likelihood of differential patterns of participation" ("Another Look at the Life Cycle," p. 761).

40. Jeane J. Kirkpatrick, *Political Woman* (New York: Basic Books, 1974),

p. 67. See also Angus Campbell, et al., *The American Voter: An Abridgement* (New York: Wiley, 1964), p. 258, where they write, in part, "The presence of young children requiring constant attention serves as a barrier to the voting act."

41. The exceptions are voting and electoral activity for 1976; keep in mind that young people between the ages of eighteen and twenty inclusive were enfranchised nationally in 1972, with the ratification of the Twenty-Sixth Amendment.

42. Note that women with many children are the most electorally active in 1960; this group is disproportionately Catholic and may be responding to Kennedy's candidacy that year. There is no evidence that the differences in levels of participation between women with three or fewer children and women with four or more is the result of class; that is, the expectation that working-class women have more children than their middle-class counterparts and that what one sees in this difference is not the dampening effect of large numbers of children upon participation but rather the depressing impact of class. Working-class women have just as many—or just as few—children as their middle-class sisters, as the following table suggests.

Class Differences in Numbers of Children for Women for Selected Years

	1960	1964	1968	1976
none	− 1.0[a]	+ 1.6	+ 3.2	− 2.6
one	+ 2.2	+ 1.4	− 1.1	− 0.5
two	+ 3.5	− 2.0	− 3.4	− 3.6
three	− 0.5	− 3.0	− 0.1	+ 1.0
four	− 4.2	− 4.7	+ 1.4	+ 5.7

[a]Percentage difference for working-class women minus middle-class women.

Note as well that the average number of children for a family receiving Aid to Families with Dependent Children was 2.2 in 1977; see *Aid to Families with Dependent Children: A Chartbook*, Publication #79-11721, 1979, p. 4, cited in Harrell R. Rodgers, Jr., and Michael Harrington, *Unfinished Democracy* (Glenview, Ill.: Scott, Foresman, 1981), p. 421. Nor is there evidence that the differences in levels of participation between women with three or fewer children and women with four or more is the result of educational differences; that is, that poorly educated women have more children than well-educated women, and hence this is what creates participation differences between women with few (or no) children and women with many children. For examples, women with four or more children who have only a grade school education account for 8.7 percent of all grade school educated women in 1960, 7.7 percent in 1964, and 4.8 percent in 1968; while women with four or more children who have some college education account for 7.8 percent of all college educated women in 1960, 10.1 percent in 1964, and 5.7 percent in 1968. Apparently mothers of many children are as likely (in these samples) to be well educated as they are to be poorly educated.

43. See Kirkpatrick, *Political Woman*; and Marcia Manning Lee, "Why Few Women Hold Public Office," *Political Science Quarterly*, Vol. 91 (2), Summer 1976, pp. 297–314.

44. For an example of this kind of study, see Murray Levine's account of the experience of women in the Love Canal neighborhood in New York State, whose political activism was responsible for the discovery of the chemical dump there and for publicizing the issue to encourage state action on the matter, in "Method or Madness: On the Alienation of the Professional," an invited address to the Annual Meetings of the American Psychological Association, Montreal, September 1–5, 1980.

45. See again Lee, "Why Few Women Hold Public Office."

46. Note that there is no control variable for marital status in 1952 or for class in 1956.

—————————————————————

CHAPTER IV

WOMEN'S POLITICAL HISTORY AND THE EXPERIENCE OF FEMINIST GENERATIONS

—————————————————————

Women's political history in the United States has been considerably different from men's. American women did not obtain full electoral citizenship until 1920, with the ratification of the Nineteenth Amendment, which enfranchised women. Political science literature has given nodding recognition to the importance of the lateness of this enfranchisement, at least in regard to the "depressed" voting levels of older women.[1]

Women's political history also includes the rise and fall of feminist movements; within this century, two major feminist movements have mobilized: the first culminated in women's suffrage, and the second the United States is still experiencing. Because we can identify a women's political history in the United States, tied to generational experience, we have an excellent opportunity for assessing the *unique*, potentially mobilizing impact of this political experience upon women. Since our purpose is to examine the conditions specific to the female experience and the effects of these conditions upon women's political participation, the study of women's political history and the experience of feminist generations can offer us some insight into that relationship. We need, then, to examine the impacts of feminist movements (or their absence) upon generations of women who experienced them. It is not unreasonable to suggest that women coming of age during a feminist movement should be more active in politics than those who came of age during non-feminist or anti-feminist periods.

DEFINING GENERATIONS: CONSIDERATIONS AND CAUTIONS

For the purposes of this chapter, a political generation is defined as a group of people marked by the shared experience of coming of age politically during a time of decisive, politically relevant events. "Shared experience" does not mean only conscious, collective experience but includes the fact of being a certain age during a particular historical period. This "certain age" is defined as being between seventeen and twenty-five years of age.[2] "Decisive, politically relevant event" refers to social or political issues of the period which touch or refer to that particular age group. Finally, since this work examines the political behavior of women, generations will be defined by events specific to women's political experience.

The definition is an amalgam of those offered by Karl Mannheim,[3] Rudolph Herberle,[4] and Samuel Huntington,[5] usually referred to as the "experiential" concept of generation,[6] in which "the most decisive factor in generational formation is the shared experience of an age cohort. The focus is usually on what happens to a particular cohort when it is at its most formative age."[7]

The emphasis of this definition of generation is on the *shared experience of politically developing young adults*. Huntington outlines the major components of the experiential approach: 1) generational differences are a function of experience; 2) compared to the preceding cohort, a new cohort may be either politically similar or dissimilar; 3) the change takes place in society; 4) the time periods for experiential generations are brief and irregular; and 5) the degree of generational conflict is intense.[8]

Using the experiential definition of generation, political generations of American women can be determined; throughout the twentieth century, major political and social changes have occurred which have shaped different generations of American women. Many of these changes were concurrent with, or in response to, feminist movements. Before describing these changes which define political generations of American women, it may be useful to consider the problems in doing so.

First, political generations include within them those who, while they do not experience the political event directly, nonetheless identify themselves with the generation. Second, those who come of age during the formation of a political generation may not identify with the dominant generational experience. That is, using survey research data which do not include questions concerning generational identification, it is uncertain that: 1) what is defined as a generation is, in fact, a generation, and 2) that those coming of age during that period—and only those—were identified with it. Herberle makes a similar point, writing: "To have the same experience in common integrates a generation into a social collective; but a generation may include several subdivisions, if the crucial experiences are met and mastered in different ways, for example, by different class groups."[9]

A final difficulty in defining political generations of *women*, suggested by William Chafe, is that women have relatively low levels of identification with women as a group, in contrast to the attachment other minorities[10] have to their respective groups. Chafe cites the

dialectic nature of women's group identity: they are separate, yet diffused through the larger whole; they are distinctive, yet share an identity with those who are their opposites in every group within society. It is for this reason that building group consciousness is so central to the prospect for any movement toward equality. It is also for this reason that such consciousness is so difficult to achieve and maintain.[11]

With these cautions in mind, four political generations of women can be determined, two of which are marked by the presence of feminist movements and two of which are marked by the absence of issues and movements with particular importance for women as a unique group. These generations are the following: 1) that generation which came of age before female enfranchisement; 2) that which came of age at the time of female enfranchisement; 3) that which came of age in a period when women's right to vote was established and accepted, so that this generation was always aware that women were full voting citizens; and 4) that which came of age during the late 1960s and early 1970s, when the contemporary feminist movement was born. In a sense, the first and third groups here defined constitute generations marked by an *absence* of a crucially decisive political event. The political events which define the second and fourth generations of women concern specific issues and conditions which uniquely concerned and affected women, in contrast to men. These were, for the former, the struggle which focused upon female enfranchisement and which was situated in an intense and increasingly visible debate about women's political role,[12] and, for the latter, the activity and debate that the renaissance of the feminist movement engendered on issues of equal civil and human rights.

Two generations are marked by events that are particularly feminist in nature and that may have encouraged participation in political life.

The other two generations are marked by an indifference or even hostility to women's political participation. The periods during which each generation came of age are: 1) the first generation, 1910 or before; 2) the second generation, 1911 to 1926; 3) the third generation, 1927 to 1960; and 4) the fourth generation, 1961 to 1976. These groupings roughly correspond to generational periods marked by political events of concern to women rather than men, in that these events have had a direct impact upon women's political and economic rights.

The First Feminist Generation: 1911–1926

The first feminist generation came of age roughly between the years 1911 and 1926, a period which saw several important social and political changes. There was a steady increase in the numbers of women employed in the work force and an increase in the numbers and percentages of women graduating from college.[13] Trade unions whose memberships were predominantly female developed and grew.[14] In 1903, the National Women's Trade Union League was formed,[15] and Women in Industry Service, the precursor of the Women's Bureau of the Department of Labor, was established in 1918. In 1919, the National Federation of Business and Professional Women's Clubs was founded.

The years 1906 to 1913 were marked by slow progress on the federal amendment to enfranchise women, according to Eleanor Flexner, although activity on the amendment continued, but the "turn of the tide" came in the years 1917 and 1918;[16] the amendment was ratified in 1920. The continuous activity and agitation on behalf of women's suffrage throughout this period were marked by several visible, flamboyant events: the founding of the National Women's Party;[17] the mass picketing by suffragists of the White House in 1917; the founding of the Women's Political Union under the leadership of Harriet Stanton Blach, as part of the National American Women's Suffrage Association (NAWSA) in 1907; and the election of Jeanette Rankin of Wyoming as the first female member of Congress in 1917. The year before her election, the Democratic Party created within itself a women's division, and the Republican Party followed in 1918.[18] The women's suffrage amendment had been brought before Congress in every year from 1896 to 1913 and was submitted again in 1919 when Congress formally proposed the amendment. In 1919, as the NAWSA dispersed with the success of the Nineteenth Amendment, the League of Women Voters was established to educate women about their new political rights.

The Second Feminist Generation: 1961–1976

The decade of the 1960s was marked by increased progressive political activity on many levels. The years 1961 to 1976 define a second feminist period, marked in 1963 by the publication of Betty Friedan's *The Feminine Mystique*,[19] which chronicled the anti-feminist spirit and culture of the preceding decades. The Equal Pay Act was passed the same year, having been one of the recommendations of the Presidential Commission on the Status of Women established by President John F. Kennedy in 1961. In November 1963, Kennedy established the Interdepartmental Committee on the Status of Women and the Citizens' Advisory Council on the Status of Women. The next year the Civil Rights Act passed with Title VII included to prevent employment discrimination on the basis of sex as well as on the basis of race.[20]

The 1960s continued to be marked by legislation beneficial to women, as well as by the founding of several feminist political organizations. These included, among many others, the National Organization for Women (1966); New York Radical Women (1967); the Women's Equity Action League, Federally Employed Women, and the Women's International Terrorist Conspiracy from Hell (1968, the year of the anti-Miss America Pageant protests in Atlantic City); the Stanton-Anthony Brigade of the New York Radical Feminists (1969); the National Women's Political Caucus (1971); the National Black Feminist Organization (1973); and the Coalition of Labor Union Women (1974).

In 1970, the first Women's Studies Program was founded at San Diego State College, followed by the development of similar programs at other universities.[21] In 1972, Shirley Chisholm was the first woman nominated for the presidential candidacy of a major political party; *Ms.* magazine published its first issue; and the Equal Rights Amendment, first presented to Congress in 1920, was formally proposed by Congress. In 1973, the Supreme Court affirmed the right of women to choose abortion, without state interference, for the first trimester.

The feminist political activity of the 1960s and 1970s was extensive and various, ranging from the informal consciousness-raising groups to abortion counseling clinics (similar to draft counseling clinics in which many women had been involved) to legislative lobbying to litigation to major political organizing around feminist issues in both major political parties. This activity has been extensive and visible, and it is reasonable to assume that young women coming of age politically during these years were influenced by these events and that they constitute a feminist political generation.[22]

The First Non-Feminist Generation: 1910 and Before

The decades between the end of the Civil War and the last and successful mobilization for women's suffrage were not completely devoid of feminist organizing. The first demand for women's suffrage, in fact, was issued in the 1848 Seneca Falls *Declaration of Rights and Sentiments* (the provision, written by Elizabeth Cady Stanton, was considered too radical and was included in the document only after a fight—and after Stanton's husband left town in protest).[23] But while feminist activity occurred prior to 1911, the ratification of the Fifteenth Amendment and the fight that took place concerning the enfranchisement of black men had served to divide the suffrage movement. As a result, "from 1870 to 1910, the suffragists were remarkably unsuccessful. This was partly due to their own conservative tactics and racist, elitist positions, which alienated their potential allies. Partly, too, it was due to continued opposition from those who feared women's votes."[24]

During the period before 1911, the suffrage movement had split over the issue of enfranchisement of black men and the exclusion of women from the Fifteenth Amendment, creating the National (1869) and the American (1870) Women's Suffrage Associations, which served to weaken the women's suffrage movement.[25] The organizations merged in 1890. It is unlikely that during this period masses of women would have been aware of feminist activity or influenced by it.

The Second Non-Feminist Generation: 1927–1960

The years from 1927 to 1960 represent what Deckard refers to as "Forty Years in the Desert." This period saw the collapse of the organized women's movement with the advent of women's suffrage. While the early 1920s included the passage of a variety of progressive social legislation, by the 1930s feminism was a dormant concern. "In the 1930s, the Great Depression politically awakened and radicalized millions of women. But their central concern was full employment, not women's rights; so they joined existing movements from the New Deal Democrats to the CIO to the Socialist and Communist Parties."[26]

While women's employment levels jumped in the late 1930s and early 1940s in response to the need for increased production to prepare the nation for war, these levels dropped dramatically in the immediate postwar period.[27] There were similar changes in education. The percent of bachelor's degrees awarded to women, which had been rising steadily since the 1890s, dropped from 41.0 in 1940 to 23.9 in 1950.[28] The cultural "sell" that accompanied the decrease in numbers of women employed outside the home and graduating from college is well documented by Friedan.[29]

Deckard argues that "there was no significant women's liberation movement in the forty years from the mid-1920s to the mid 1960s" because 1) the old suffrage organizations were focusing on education and issues which were not primarily women's issues and 2) left-wing parties advocating women's rights were being persecuted.[30] Whatever the reasons, the years from 1927 to 1960 can indeed be described as forty years in the desert for American feminism and cannot be expected to have produced a generation of women with the sense that women should participate fully and equally in political life.[31]

The four women's political generations described above result in two generations which are relatively feminist and two that are not. Women coming of age politically between the years 1911 and 1926 grew up during the period of a visible women's rights struggle and at a time when women were entering the work force and attending institutions of higher education in increasing numbers. Women of this generation are expected to be more likely to participate in politics than their counterparts of the previous generation, where there was neither a strong women's movement nor the example of large numbers of women entering the public sphere.

Women coming of age politically after 1960 are also expected to be more active politically than their counterparts of the preceding generation. The advent of a feminist movement renaissance is expected to have affected the women who came of age after 1960 by encouraging their participation in politics.

GENERATION AND PARTICIPATION

Table 16 gives the absolute numbers and percentages of women in each generation across the seven years under study. All the variables for age are recoded either from actual reported age or birth date data.

Table 16.
Distribution (Percent and Total Number) of Respondents across Political Generations, 1952–1976

	1952	1956	1960	1964	1968	1972	1976
GENERATION 1.	14.8% (262)	11.7% (206)	9.8% (116)	5.1% (80)	2.9% (45)	1.3% (35)	0.3% (10)
GENERATION 2.	26.2 (464)	32.3 (568)	23.6 (278)	18.5 (290)	17.5 (273)	12.2 (328)	9.9 (282)
GENERATION 3.	59.1 (1047)	55.9 (983)	66.5 (785)	68.6 (1075)	63.2 (984)	53.9 (1449)	48.1 (1372)
GENERATION 4.	0.0 (0)	0.0 (0)	0.1 (1)	7.7 (121)	16.4 (255)	32.9 (876)	41.6 (1186)

Note:

Generation 1. includes all those who came of age (reached their twenty-first birthday) before 1911. Generation 2. includes all those who came of age between 1911 and 1926, inclusive. Generation 3. includes all those who came of age between 1927 and 1960, inclusive. Generation 4. includes all those who came of age after 1960.

Comparisons among different generations of women, using ICPSR data, are problematic at best, given the confounding factor of age. For example, the youngest member of the first generation was seventy-four years old in 1964, while her third-generation counterpart was only fifty-eight. While the traditional effects of age upon participation may contaminate relationships between generation and activism, effective controls for age are impossible to apply across the range of these four generations, since there are so few women of similar age and dissimilar generation for any sample years. Our alternative, imperfect but still useful, is simply to compare generations across the seven sample years, regardless of incomparability of respondents' ages, to assess how membership in a feminist, rather than a non-feminist, movement affects women's participation.

In order to confirm the hypothesis that membership in a feminist political generation had a positive impact upon women's political participation, the following should be evident in the data. First, among women, there should be an alternating effect across generations within each data year, with women in the first and third (non-feminist) generations participating less than their sisters in the second and fourth (feminist) generations. Again, some age related influence may mask an oscillation, so we may not completely reject a generational explanation, but even a modest alternation between greater and lesser activism in response to the presence and absence of a feminist movement would hint at a stronger but hidden relationship. Second, there should be no such effect for men, given that these generational groupings are based on events considered unique to women.

Table 17 presents participation data for women and men, by generation, for the years 1952 to 1976. For none of the forms of participation considered is there a clear alternating effect; that is, participation among women is not higher for the second and fourth (feminist) generations than it is for the first and third (non-feminist) generations.

First, there is no consistent voting pattern among women that would demonstrate any generational effects. In fact, a better case might be made for the traditional effects of age,[32] since voting participation is greatest for those generations whose members are middle-aged (second and third generations), rather than for those whose members are either very old (first generation) or very young (fourth generation).

Nor does there seem to be any generation related electoral participation[33] among women. Except for women of the first genera-

Table 17.
Percent Active, and Total Number of, Women and Men, by Generation, 1952–1976

	1952		1956		1960		1964		1968		1972		1976	
	Women	Men	Women	Men	Women	Men	Women	Men	Women	Men	Women	Men	Women	Men
VOTING														
Generation 1.	95.2% (126)	98.1% (108)	66.1% (112)	85.9% (99)	66.1% (59)	71.9% (57)	78.0% (41)	*	59.3% (27)	*	*	*	*	*
Generation 2.	96.6 (232)	97.9 (194)	74.8 (286)	83.0 (282)	74.1 (147)	85.5 (131)	72.0 (157)	86.7 (113)	69.9 (133)	82.1 (106)	64.0 (186)	75.5 (94)	56.0 (151)	86.4 (81)
Generation 3.	97.0 (503)	98.4 (429)	64.2 (573)	75.6 (405)	73.8 (439)	82.7 (346)	78.4 (547)	81.1 (460)	80.2 (494)	80.5 (384)	75.3 (693)	81.7 (535)	76.0 (660)	84.5 (510)
Generation 4.	*	*	*	*	*	*	59.0 (61)	56.8 (44)	58.1 (129)	67.6 (105)	65.2 (405)	68.2 (330)	61.6 (585)	65.5 (394)
ELECTORAL PARTICIPATION														
Generation 1.	4.8% (125)	15.7% (108)	6.2% (112)	16.2% (99)	7.3% (55)	12.0% (50)	9.8% (41)	*	*	*	*	*	*	*
Generation 2.	9.5 (232)	13.1 (191)	14.0 (286)	18.9 (281)	16.7 (132)	20.0 (125)	14.1 (156)	20.9 (110)	14.4 (125)	17.2 (99)	9.8 (183)	11.2 (89)	10.9 (151)	7.0 (79)
Generation 3.	8.8 (499)	12.4 (248)	13.7 (570)	14.9 (404)	18.3 (409)	18.2 (325)	15.7 (540)	18.6 (458)	16.3 (466)	18.9 (359)	17.1 (650)	21.9 (515)	14.4 (610)	20.7 (460)
Generation 4.	*	*	*	*	*	*	8.3 (60)	4.7 (43)	15.6 (122)	12.9 (101)	16.0 (394)	18.0 (317)	12.8 (536)	11.1 (347)

*N < 20.   Note: Generation 1 includes all those who came of age (reached the age of twenty-one) before 1911; Generation 2 includes all those who came of age between 1911 and 1926, inclusive; Generation 3 includes all those who came of age between 1927 and 1960, inclusive; and Generation 4 includes all those who came of age after 1960.

84

	1952		1956		1960		1964		1968		1972		1976	
	Women	Men	Women	Men	Women	Men	Women	Men	Women	Men	Women	Men	Women	Men
CONVENTIONAL ACTIVISM														
Generation 1.	*	*	*	*	*	*	12.2% (41)	*	16.0% (25)	*	*	*	*	*
Generation 2.	*	*	*	*	*	*	16.0 (156)	23.9 (113)	11.0 (127)	23.3 (103)	18.6 (183)	26.1 (88)	11.7 (150)	24.4 (80)
Generation 3.	*	*	*	*	*	*	18.9 (546)	20.5 (459)	20.0 (479)	25.7 (369)	30.0 (651)	33.3 (516)	30.2 (650)	26.8 (507)
Generation 4.	*	*	*	*	*	*	8.2 (61)	6.8 (44)	16.8 (125)	18.0 (100)	26.6 (394)	25.8 (318)	26.7 (581)	31.3 (393)
UNCONVENTIONAL ACTIVISM														
Generation 1.	*	*	*	*	*	*	*	*	*	*	*	*	*	*
Generation 2.	*	*	*	*	*	*	*	*	7.1 (98)	9.0 (78)	1.6 (187)	1.9 (106)	1.6 (186)	6.2 (97)
Generation 3.	*	*	*	*	*	*	*	*	12.1 (49)	14.8 (50)	5.7 (779)	4.3 (609)	9.8 (74)	11.0 (67)
Generation 4.	*	*	*	*	*	*	*	*	26.2 (107)	19.4 (93)	9.9 (467)	15.4 (395)	16.4 (698)	17.1 (487)

*N < 20.

Note: Generation 1 includes all those who came of age (reached the age of twenty-one) before 1911; Generation 2 includes all those who came of age between 1911 and 1926, inclusive; Generation 3 includes all those who came of age between 1927 and 1960, inclusive: and Generation 4 includes all those who came of age after 1960.

Unconventional activism for 1968 and 1972 represents support for such activities; the variable for 1976 represents actual unconventional participation.

Table 17 (continued)

	1952		1956		1960		1964		1968		1972		1976	
	Women	Men	Women	Men	Women	Men	Women	Men	Women	Men	Women	Men	Women	Men
POLITICAL INVOLVEMENT														
Generation 1.	15.7% (121)	20.2% (104)	13.4% (112)	11.3% (97)	43.4% (53)	40.7% (49)	15.0% (40)	*	16.0% (25)	*	*	*	*	*
Generation 2.	23.8 (231)	35.1 (188)	13.1 (283)	18.2 (280)	34.7 (124)	43.2 (120)	25.6 (156)	26.1 (111)	20.3 (123)	22.8 (101)	22.2 (99)	25.5 (47)	18.0 (148)	23.1 (90)
Generation 3.	23.2 (492)	24.9 (418)	12.8 (564)	16.8 (399)	33.3 (389)	42.7 (312)	22.6 (540)	17.9 (455)	21.2 (468)	24.7 (364)	24.3 (334)	33.0 (261)	26.0 (651)	28.8 (506)
Generation 4.	*	*	*	*	*	*	11.5 (61)	18.2 (44)	13.7 (124)	23.0 (100)	17.5 (194)	23.7 (156)	15.7 (581)	23.1 (388)
POLITICAL EFFICACY														
Generation 1.	14.6 (137)	33.1 (118)	23.9 (109)	34.0 (94)	27.1 (59)	28.3 (53)	14.6 (48)	32.1 (28)	33.3 (27)	*	*	*	*	*
Generation 2.	20.1 (254)	39.2 (204)	31.9 (282)	46.4 (276)	39.9 (138)	50.4 (127)	25.0 (164)	31.6 (117)	36.2 (149)	52.1 (121)	13.5 (208)	26.3 (114)	21.3 (146)	14.7 (75)
Generation 3.	24.0 (549)	36.9 (462)	30.9 (564)	43.3 (404)	35.7 (426)	51.2 (340)	28.5 (571)	40.5 (487)	53.4 (536)	63.7 (422)	23.5 (812)	33.8 (624)	19.6 (650)	40.1 (505)
Generation 4.	*	*	*	*	*	*	30.8 (65)	34.6 (52)	57.4 (141)	69.4 (111)	20.0 (475)	33.8 (400)	23.7 (567)	32.3 (390)

*N < 20.

Note: Generation 1 includes all those who came of age (reached the age of twenty-one) before 1911; Generation 2 includes all those who came of age between 1911 and 1926, inclusive; Generation 3 includes all those who came of age between 1927 and 1960, inclusive; and Generation 4 includes all those who came of age after 1960.

Question-wording in the 1968 survey exaggerates the proportion of efficacious respondents.

tion, women's electoral participation is similar across generations for most years. Women of the second, third, and fourth generations are electorally active at about the same levels, despite age differences, with few exceptions. It may be, however, that the "exception" of women of the first (non-feminist) generation points to a more important generation related difference, that of the date of women's enfranchisement. The real generational line might be drawn between those who came of age before women's suffrage and those who came of age after, regardless of succeeding feminist movements. This possibility will be discussed later.

An assessment of the relationship between generation and conventional participation[34] is further limited by the availability of data. Questions concerning conventional participation were first included in ICPSR surveys in 1964; hence, there are few women and no men from the first generation remaining in the sample. Again, however, there is little evidence of generation related participation differences among women. Aside from 1964, for women of the fourth generation (which appears for the first time in the 1964 survey), the similarities among women across generations are more striking than the differences.

Women's participation in unconventional political activity[35] likewise does not demonstrate the expected generational differences; rather, support for unconventional activism and actual unconventional political participation increases with each generation, with the fourth (feminist) generation being most supportive of unconventional activity in 1968 and 1972 and most participant in 1976. In fact, the percentage of activists for the fourth generation is twice as great, in all years, as the next most active generation. While the difference between women in this fourth generation from women of preceding generations may indicate simply an age related effect, it is nonetheless likely that another "generational line," much like that of women's suffrage, exists. Again, this possibility will be discussed later in this chapter.

Women's political involvement[36] also seems independent of a generation related explanation. There are not the expected alternating levels of participation across generation within years, especially in regard to expected differences between the second (feminist) and third (non-feminist) generations, whose levels of involvement are strikingly similar. The greatest difference in involvement between women of these two generations comes in 1976, when 8 percent more of the third-generation women are involved than their second-generation counter-

parts. An interesting anomaly in generation related political involvement is that of the fourth-generation women. These women enter the
survey in 1964 and, not surprisingly, demonstrate the lowest levels of
political involvement for that year, relative to that of other generations. However, this low ranking does not change as this generation
of women matures, as we might expect. Instead, women of the fourth
generation remain consistently the least politically involved of all generations for the years 1964 to 1976. Again, this suggests that important generational differences may exist, in addition to those suggested
thus far.

Finally, generational differences appear to be unrelated to feelings
of political efficacy,[37] with this exception: women of the first (non-
feminist) generation consistently report the smallest proportions of efficacious women. While we cannot claim that this is *not* the result of
age, rather than generation, it seems logical that a group of women
who became adults when "people like them" had no formal, legal
relationship to politics might well feel that politics is too complicated
to understand. However, women of the second, third, and fourth generations have relatively similar levels of political efficacy; the greatest
similarities exist between women of the second (feminist) and third
(non-feminist) generations from 1952 to 1964, while the third (non-
feminist) and fourth (feminist) generations appear most similar from
1968 to 1976. Again, the relationship between generation and political
efficacy does not support our original hypothesis.

Finally, our argument also rests on our claim that exposure to a
feminist generation should have a positive, *unique* impact upon wom-
en's participation, one not evident for men. Again, our data do not
permit us to reject with certainty any relationship, but they may suggest possibilities for acceptance. For the generation related participation hypothesis to be accepted, not only must women of the second
and fourth (feminist) generations participate more than their counterparts in the first and third (non-feminist) generations, but the differences between women must be greater than the differences between
men.[38] An examination of gender related participation differences across
generation (see Table 17) shows that the generation related hypothesis
can be accepted at least as frequently for *men* as for women. There is
more generational alternation of participation for men than there is for
women. Since the age factor does not contaminate comparisons of

gender related difference, this evidence more firmly rejects our claim that exposure to a feminist generation has a unique and positive impact upon women's mass-level political participation.

In the previous discussion of the data in Table 17, several exceptions to the general pattern of generational similarity were noted. First, women of the first (non-feminist) generation reported consistently less electoral activism as well as consistently fewer feelings of political efficacy. Second, women of the fourth (feminist) generation reported consistently more support for unconventional activism (as well as more actual unconventional participation), while at the same time they reported less political involvement. It was suggested that generational lines might not be consistent across all types of participation but rather that there might be key types of behavior that are delineated by generation. The suggestion that generation may have had a unique impact upon the electoral participation or efficacy of the first generation, however, is not borne out by the data. While it is true that these women are distinguished from their sisters by relatively low levels of electoral activism and feelings of political efficacy, their male counterparts are likewise distinguished from their brothers of succeeding generations. In none of the years under study is the difference in feelings of political efficacy between women of the first generation and the succeeding second generation greater than the difference between their male equivalents. For electoral activism, differences between women are greater than differences between men only for 1952 and 1956. Again, since the impact of the first (non-feminist) generation seems to be similar for women and men, the generational hypothesis is rejected.

Our conclusions are similar for women of the fourth (feminist) generation, at least with regard to unconventional activism. Table 17 shows that women of this generation are more supportive of, and more active in, unconventional activism than women of the second (feminist) or third (non-feminist) generations.[39] However, the same pattern holds true for men of the fourth generation. In 1968 and in 1976, differences in unconventional activism between women of the fourth and third generations were greater than the differences between men—but the difference is only 0.7 percent in 1976, and the differences between men are greater than the differences between women in 1972. Again, women and men are behaving more similarly than differently, which argues against the generational hypothesis for women.

In the case of political involvement, however, women of the fourth (feminist) generation report less political involvement than their third-generation sisters, from 1964 (when the fourth-generation respondents entered the sample) to 1976. In addition, the low levels of political involvement among fourth-generation women are not matched by their male fourth-generation counterparts. The differences in political involvement between fourth-generation and third-generation women are greater than the differences between fourth-generation and third-generation men. However, low levels of political involvement among fourth-generation women run in the opposite direction of the hypothesis: that women coming of age during the contemporary feminist movement would, because of that experience, be more involved in politics than their counterparts coming of age during non-feminist or anti-feminist decades. This may suggest that political involvement marks the single most important behavioral differnce between women growing up in different generations and that the contemporary feminist movement and changes in the status of women have had the effect of depressing levels of political involvement among women who came of age with the movement.

CONCLUSION

We have little evidence to support the hypothesis of generational difference. There is no increase in participation among women from the ''least feminist'' (first, third) generations to the ''most feminist'' (second, fourth), and in few cases are there any generational differences worth noting. Women's participation across generations is more similar than it is dissimilar, even with the complicating factor of age differences, and women's and men's participation across generations demonstrates similar patterns. However, while we must reject the claim that exposure to a feminist generation has a *unique* impact upon women's participation, we cannot jettison the idea that membership in a feminist generation has *no* impact upon women's participation. Other data sets may provide confirmation of a positive (if not unique) relationship between generation and participation for women which these data do not permit us to embrace. Particular types of activism for certain generations—voting and political efficacy for first-generation women and unconventional activism and political involvement for fourth-generation women—would be excellent foci for further research.

NOTES

1. For a discussion of women's suffrage and women's voting participation, see: Angus Campbell et al., *The American Voter: An Abridgement* (New York: Wiley, 1964), pp. 255–259; Norman H. Nie, Sidney Verba, and John R. Petrocik, *The Changing American Voter* (Cambridge, Mass.: Harvard University Press, 1976), pp. 77, 89, and 90–91; and Marjorie Lansing, "The American Woman: Voter and Activist," in Jane S. Jaquette, ed., *Women in Politics* (New York: Wiley, 1974), pp. 5–24.

2. Karl Mannheim, "The Problem of Generations," *Essays on the Sociology of Knowledge* (London: Routledge and Kegan Paul, 1952).

3. Ibid., pp. 288–289.

4. Rudolph Heberle, *Social Movements: An Introduction to Political Sociology* (New York: Appleton-Century-Crofts, 1951), p. 119.

5. Samuel Huntington, "Generations, Cycles, and Their Role in American Development," pp. 11–12, in Richard J. Samuels, ed., *Political Generations and Political Development* (Lexington, Mass.: Lexington Books, 1977).

6. Ibid., p. 12.

7. Mannheim, "The Problem of Generations," pp. 288–289.

8. Huntington, "Generations," p. 12.

9. Heberle, *Social Movements*, p. 124.

10. Despite the fact that in the modern United States, women constitute a numerical majority, William Chafe argues that a minority group model is applicable to women. "The minority group model is perhaps most helpful in the emphasis it places on separate institutions and on a distinctive group identity as a basis for interaction with the dominant culture. . . . Women . . . have scored the greatest gains for equal rights and social reform when they have created their own institutions." William Chafe, *Women and Equality: Changing Patterns in American Culture* (New York: Oxford University Press, 1967), p. 175, emphasis in original. Chafe uses Louis Wirth's definition of a minority group:

"a group of people who, because of their physical or cultural characteristics, are singled out from the others in the society in which they live for differential and unequal treatment." Wirth noted that minorities could not be judged by number alone, because on occasion they constituted a numerical majority. Rather they were distinguished by their exclusion from full participation in society, their debarment from certain economic, political, and social opportunities, "the restricted scope of their occupational and professional advancement," and the general tendency to treat them as "members of a category, irrespective of their individual merits." There seems to be little question that on the basis of these characteristics, women qualify as a minority group. (p. 4).

11. Ibid., p. 176. The definition here cannot speak to generational consciousness because of the lack of appropriate data.

12. Women's political role was seen by some during the period of the

suffrage movement as that of purifying politics, of introducing the morality of the home into the public sphere. Prohibition was an example of the kind of issue women's new role was expected to address. For a discussion of the purifying element of women's suffrage, see Jean Bethke Elshtain, "Moral Woman and Immoral Man: A Consideration of the Public-Private Split and Its Political Ramifications," *Politics and Society*, IV (4), Summer 1974, pp. 453–473; Aileen Kraditor, *The Ideas of the Women's Suffrage Movement, 1890–1920* (New York: Anchor Books, 1971), Chapter V, "Women and the Home"; and Carol Hymowitz and Michaele Weissman, *A History of Women in America* (New York: Bantam Books, 1978), pp. 184–185.

13.   Women earned 18.9 percent of all degrees conferred in 1900 and 39.5 percent in 1930. They accounted for 19.1 percent of all bachelor's degrees conferred in 1900 and 39.8 in 1930; 19.1 percent of all master's degrees conferred in 1900 and 40.4 percent in 1930 went to women. See *Handbook on Women Workers* (Washington, D.C.: U.S. Government Printing Office, 1969), p. 191.

14.   Eleanor Flexner, *Century of Struggle* (Cambridge, Mass.: Belknap Press, 1975), p. 248.

15.   Barbara Deckard gives the date as 1903. See Barbara Deckard, *The Women's Movement: Political, Socioeconomic, and Psychological Issues* (New York: Harper and Row, 1975), p. 269.

16.   Flexner, *Century of Struggle*, Chapter XXI.

17.   Flexner gives the date as 1916; Deckard, as 1914.

18.   Deckard, *The Women's Movement*, pp. 291–292.

19.   Betty Friedan, *The Feminine Mystique* (New York: Dell, 1964).

20.   For an excellent discussion of the clause including women as a protected class, see Jo Freeman, *The Politics of Women's Liberation* (New York: David McKay, 1975), pp. 53–54.

21.   These included the State University of New York at Buffalo, the University of Michigan at Ann Arbor, the University of New Hampshire, Stanford University, Rutgers University, Cornell University, and the University of Wisconsin at Madison, among many others.

22.   For a feminist chronology, see Redstockings of the Women's Liberation Movement, "Concrete Accomplishments," in *Feminist Revolution: An Abridged Edition* (New York: Random House, 1978), p. 169; and "The Decade of Women," *Ms.*, December 1979, pp. 60–94.

23.   See Miriam Gurko, *The Ladies of Seneca Falls* (New York: Schocken, 1976), Chapter 10, especially pp. 98–99.

24.   Deckard gives amazingly short shrift to the betrayal of female suffragists over the issue of black male enfranchisement as a cause for the "lack of success" the women's suffrage movement suffered after 1870 and considerably underestimates the hostile and well-financed opposition to the enfranchise-

ment of women by big business, especially the breweries, political machines, and immigrant and racist groups. For a more sophisticated account of the causes of the failure of the women's suffrage movement after 1870, see any one of the following: Flexner, *Century of Struggle*; Hymowitz and Weissman, *History of Women*; William O'Neill, *Everyone Was Brave: The Rise and Fall of Feminism in America* (Chicago: Quadrangle, 1969); and Gurko, *Ladies of Seneca Falls*.

25. Hymowitz and Weissman, *History of Women*, write: "The split lasted for twenty years. The divisions between the two groups went far deeper than the clash between votes for blacks and votes for women. The basic disagreement concerned the means and ends of the women's movement." (p. 160) The AWSA was reformist and concerned with the suffrage issue. The NWSA had a broader and more radical vision (at least while Elizabeth Cady Stanton was alive) of the goals and tactics of the movement.

26. Deckard, *The Women's Movement*, p. 294.

27. Women constituted 25.4 percent of the entire labor force in March 1940 (pre-World War II), 36.1 percent in April 1945, 27.6 percent in April 1947 (post-World War II), and 29.1 percent in April 1950. See *Handbook on Women Workers*, Table 1, p. 10.

28. Ibid., p. 191.

29. Friedan, *Feminine Mystique*, Chapter 2.

30. Deckard, *The Women's Movement*, p. 321.

31. Ethel Klein suggests that this awareness comes later, with the conflict between women's life experience (education, employment) and their traditional expectations about woman's role. See Ethel Klein, *Gender Politics* (Cambridge, Mass.: Harvard University Press, 1984), Chapter Five.

32. For a discussion of the relationship between age and women's voting participation, see Raymond E. Wolfinger and Steven J. Rosenstone, *Who Votes?* (New Haven: Yale University Press, 1980), Chapter 3: "Age and Sex."

33. Electoral activism is measured as an index of three variables: attending political meetings, working for a political campaign or candidate, and contributing money.

34. Conventional participation is measured as an index containing variables of writing letters to public officials and to newspapers. For a full description of this index, see Chapter II, p. 29.

35. Unconventional political participation is measured as an index of support for protest activities, conscientious objection, and civil disobedience (for 1968 and 1972) and as an index of petition, protest, and sit-in activity for 1976. See Chapter II, pp. 29–30, for a full description of these indices.

36. Political involvement is measured as an index of attentiveness to political campaigns and use of the print media. This index is fully described in Chapter II, pp. 30–31.

37. Political efficacy is measured by disagreement with the following statement: "Sometimes politics and government seem so complicated that a person like me can't understand what's going on."

38. Men might evidence the same differences in participation as women, across generation, but for different reasons; this would require a detailed explanation of what those motivations might be and a data set appropriate to testing that explanation, both of which are beyond the scope of this study.

39. There were no data available for first-generation women by 1968, when questions about unconventional activism were first included in ICPSR surveys.

CHAPTER V

FEMINISM AND POLITICAL PARTICIPATION

The advent of the contemporary feminist movement has been marked by two developments of importance to women's political participation. First, the feminist movement has attempted to redefine and develop a feminist ideology, to analyze critically women's role in society, and to guide the movement's strategies for bringing about change.[1] Second, as part of the movement's political development, it has attempted to foster a sense of group identity or feminist solidarity, otherwise known as "sisterhood."

In this chapter, the relationship between feminism and women's political participation will be investigated, in an attempt to assess both the effects of support for feminist ideology and of identification with feminism as a social movement. This requires a consideration of what feminist issues and feminist identification are, how they can be operationalized using ICPSR data, and in what particular or unique ways they might be related to women's political participation rather than to men's.

FEMINISM AS GROUP IDENTITY

One of the successes of the contemporary feminist movement has been its development, among large numbers of women, of a sense of identification with the movement, that is, its ability to promote group identification among women.[2] The feminist movement in the United States has had its successes not only through feminist organizational membership, but as a result of mobilizing women on the basis of group identity; the movement has promoted group identity through its political strategy of consciousness-raising.[3]

It is expected that feminist group identity among women will be positively related to women's political participation, as the case has been for group identity and participation for others.[4] Verba and Nie found that group identity was an important predictor of political participation. In their examination of black political participation, they found that group identity was an important predictor of participation among blacks (at least for certain forms of political participation):

The most significant fact is that the [black-white] gap in participation can be so completely closed by the awareness of group identity. Those who argue for the potency of symbols such as Black Power and the need to create cohesion among blacks as a step toward full participation in society would find support for their position in these data.[5]

Arthur Miller and others argue that "group consciousness" is a more useful concept for predicting political participation, although they caution that "few people . . . conveyed a high degree of group consciousness."[6] They found the same positive relationship between group consciousness and participation that Verba and Nie found between group identity and participation, writing: "group attitudes act to stimulate political participation among an important segment of the population—the disadvantaged. Without the mobilizing influence of group consciousness, these strata would clearly participate at significantly lower rates."[7]

It is expected that feminist group identity will have a similarly positive impact upon women's political participation and that an indicator of "closeness to women's liberation" offers the best chance of revealing participation differences based upon differences in feminist group identity. Those who identify themselves closely with women's liberation are expected to be more active politically than those who are neutral to, or who do not identify with, the feminist movement.

The ICPSR data contain questions of support for the women's liberation movement, for 1972 and 1976. Responses to the 1972 question are measured on a seven-point scale, from strong approval of the women's liberation movement to strong disapproval. Responses to the

1976 question are measured on a feeling thermometer, ranging from extremely warm feelings towards women's liberation to extremely cold feelings.[8] On the basis of these questions, respondents were grouped into "identifiers" and "nonidentifiers": where identifiers are those who strongly support the women's liberation movement (1972) or feel extremely warmly toward the movement (1976); nonidentifiers are everyone else. Since there are no data that specifically tap group identity, these questions have been recoded "stringently": identifiers in 1972 are all respondents giving the highest possible approval to the women's liberation movement, and identifiers in 1976 are all respondents who rated their feelings of warmth toward women's liberation at eighty-five or higher.

Tables 18, 19, and 20 show the distribution of activism for feminist group identifiers and nonidentifiers, for women and men. If a feminist group identification is positively related to political participation, the following should be evident. First, women who identify with the women's liberation movement should participate more than women who do not identify with it. Second, feminist group identification is considered specific to women and not to men; that is, men who give high approval ratings to the feminist movement or who feel very warmly toward women's liberation are considered here as giving support to issues, rather than as demonstrating identification with a group. Therefore, men who are "identifiers" should show few differences in participation in contrast with men who are not identifiers; that is, feminist group identification among men should make little or no difference to male political participation.[9] Tables 18 through 20 show the distribution of activism for feminist identification for both sexes; the relationship between feminist group identity and participation is controlled for the level of education of the respondent.

These tables suggest the following. First, the relationship between feminist group identity and political participation is neither consistent nor strong. Second, positive relationships between feminist group identity and participation among women seem to be the province of the college educated. Third, feminist identity in many cases makes as much contribution to political participation among men as it does among women.

Table 18 gives some evidence that feminist group identification among college educated women is positively related to some forms of political participation but not others. There are large differences in partici-

Table 18.

Percent Active, and Total Number of, College Educated Women and Men, by Feminist Group Identification, 1972 and 1976

	1972		1976	
	Women	Men	Women	Men
Voting				
Feminist	90.7% (43)	69.2% (26)	82.4% (54)	80.0% (28)
Nonfeminist	88.4 (242)	83.7 (264)	84.8 (326)	84.7 (317)
Electoral activism				
Feminist	46.5 (43)	23.1 (26)	28.2 (52)	34.7 (25)
Nonfeminist	26.0 (242)	26.5 (264)	24.2 (292)	18.6 (266)
Conventional activism				
Feminist	23.2 (43)	23.1 (26)	17.6 (54)	13.1 (28)
Nonfeminist	13.3 (242)	10.6 (264)	11.8 (323)	12.8 (317)
Unconventional activism				
Feminist	48.9 (43)	52.0 (25)	16.7 (54)	30.9 (28)
Nonfeminist	21.8 (240)	23.9 (260)	18.3 (326)	22.8 (316)
Political Involvement				
Feminist	39.1 (23)	*	38.0 (54)	54.5 (28)
Nonfeminist	27.8 (133)	42.6 (129)	34.9 (325)	35.3 (316)
Political efficacy				
Feminist	48.8 (43)	46.2 (26)	38.9 (54)	48.1 (28)
Nonfeminist	35.5 (242)	45.0 (262)	31.9 (320)	47.6 (317)

*N<20.

pation between female identifiers and nonidentifiers for electoral activism, involvement, and political efficacy in 1972 and smaller differences for conventional activism and political efficacy in 1976. In each of these cases, feminist group identification makes a difference for women but not for men; that is, men's participation remains substantially the same, whether or not men report themselves as identifiers. However, in several other cases, feminist group identification makes more of a positive difference in men's participation than it does in women's (in 1976, for electoral and unconventional activism and involvement). In other cases, feminist group identification has the same impact on participation for both men and women (for examples, unconventional and conventional activism in 1976).

The relationship is similar among high school educated respondents (see Table 19).

In 1972, feminist group identification contributes more to women's participation than men's for unconventional activism, involvement, and political efficacy; and for almost all forms of participation (except perhaps for unconventional activism), participation among men is unrelated to or unaffected by feminist group identification. By 1976, however, feminist group identification has similar impacts upon both women's and men's levels of participation. In the cases of electoral activism and political efficacy for 1976, feminist group identity contributes more to men's electoral behavior and feelings of efficacy than it does to women's.

The relationship between feminist group identification and participation is weakest for those few respondents who have grade school educations (see Table 20). Among these respondents, there are few participants of either gender. Feminist group identification increases women's political participation in only one case: unconventional activism.[10] For all other types of participation, feminist group identity has either the same impact upon both women's and men's participation—or it increases men's participation but not women's.[11]

Table 21 provides information on the strength, direction, and level of statistical significance of the relationship between feminist group identity and particpation, for women and for men.

Negative coefficients indicate a positive relationship between feminist group identity and participation.[12] These data confirm the evidence in the previous tables: the relationship between feminist group consciousness and participation is not uniform; it is stronger in 1972

Table 19.

Percent Active, and Total Number of, High School Educated Women and Men, by Feminist Group Identification, 1972 and 1976

	1972		1976	
	Women	Men	Women	Men
Voting				
Feminist	68.7%	70.8%	63.4%	63.1%
	(67)	(48)	(92)	(42)
Nonfeminist	68.5	73.4	65.8	69.8
	(581)	(338)	(626)	(353)
Electoral activism				
Feminist	16.4	14.6	5.3	18.5
	(67)	(48)	(85)	(41)
Nonfeminist	13.1	13.4	10.9	11.2
	(582)	(336)	(579)	(323)
Conventional activism				
Feminist	6.0	10.4	7.2	4.9
	(67)	(48)	(91)	(41)
Nonfeminist	4.6	7.1	4.5	7.0
	(582)	(338)	(619)	(351)
Unconventional activism				
Feminist	24.1	19.1	5.5	6.0
	(66)	(47)	(92)	(42)
Nonfeminist	11.4	13.0	12.7	12.9
	(570)	(329)	(626)	(352)
Political involvement				
Feminist	25.0	20.0	20.8	23.8
	(28)	(25)	(92)	(42)
Nonfeminist	17.8	21.6	15.8	17.5
	(297)	(171)	(620)	(348)
Political efficacy				
Feminist	23.9	25.0	11.6	31.0
	(67)	(48)	(91)	(42)
Nonfeminist	19.3	29.7	19.2	25.9
	(580)	(337)	(619)	(353)

Table 20.
Percent Active, and Total Number of, Grade School Educated Women and Men, by Feminist Group Identification, 1972 and 1976

	1972		1976	
	Women	Men	Women	Men
Voting				
Feminist	62.5% (24)	77.8% (27)	*	82.5% (20)
Nonfeminist	52.2 (159)	70.5 (132)	58.4 (128)	70.8 (117)
Electoral activism				
Feminist	4.2 (24)	11.1 (27)	*	*
Nonfeminist	3.1 (159)	12.9 (132)	6.1 (124)	7.5 (114)
Conventional activism				
Feminist	0.0 (24)	0.0 (27)	*	5.0 (20)
Nonfeminist	1.9 (159)	2.3 (132)	2.0 (124)	0.9 (116)
Unconventional activism				
Feminist	15.3 (26)	9.1 (22)	*	0.0 (20)
Nonfeminist	3.5 (144)	4.0 (126)	2.0 (126)	3.0 (115)
Political involvement				
Feminist	*	*	*	*
Nonfeminist	19.5 (82)	17.6 (74)	9.8 (122)	12.6 (115)
Political efficacy				
Feminist	4.2 (24)	23.1 (26)	*	25.0 (20)
Nonfeminist	6.9 (159)	14.5 (131)	9.6 (120)	16.3 (114)

*N<20.

Table 21.
The Uncontrolled Relationship between Feminist Identification and Participation, Selected by Gender, 1972 and 1976

	1972		1976	
	Women	Men	Women	Men
Voting	-.07	.11	.01	-.03
Electoral participation	-.14[b]	.02	.03	.07
Conventional activism	-.13[b]	.06	.04[a]	.00
Unconventional activism	-.30[c]	-.16[b]	.01	.00
Political involvement	-.10[a]	-.09	-.03	.09[a]
Political efficacy	.08	.01	-.02	-.07

[a] $p < .05$.   [b] $p < .01$.   [c] $p < .001$.

Note:
     Figures are standardized regression coefficients; negative coefficients indicate a positive relationship between feminist group identification and participation. When controlled for class, race, education, and age, partial correlations show that feminist group identification contributes less than 3 percent to political activism, except in the case of unconventional activism among women in 1972, where it contributes an additional 9.4 percent. Positive coefficients for political efficacy indicate a positive relationship between feminist group identification and efficacy.

than in 1976; and it is not unique to women for all forms of participation. An examination of the partial correlation coefficients for race, class, education, and age reveals that in only one case does feminist group identification positively contribute to political participation.[13]

The relationship between feminist group identification and participation is more complex than expected: feminist group identification has an impact upon participation for the college educated, but not solely for women, not for every form of political participation, and not for every year. There may be, however, an alternative connection between feminism and participation. It may be that the feminist movement has been able to mobilize women for political action by promoting demands which have special importance to women's lives; support for feminist demands may be positively related to women's political participation. The following section considers this alternative explanation of the connection between feminism and political activism among women.

FEMINISM AS SUPPORT FOR POLITICAL ISSUES

The contemporary American feminist movement has organized itself around a series of issues which are of particular importance to women. While there are disagreements among the various branches of the movement, there are identifiable issues which the feminist movement has promoted and which serve as the basis of the movement's political demands.[14] Some feminist issues are more specific than others; some are specific policy demands, while others have been stated in more general terms. Examples of the more general political issues include civil equality, reproductive freedom, freedom from violence, economic independence, sexual freedom, and the claim that the feminist movement is the legitimate representative of masses of American women.[15]

The more specific expression of these general issues include policy demands such as the following: 1) ratification of the Equal Rights Amendment, equal employment opportunity, equal access to educational programs (varying from admissions to seminaries to admissions to skilled apprenticeship programs); 2) legalization and public funding of abortion, sex education in public schools, prohibitions against sterilization of women without their knowledge and consent, public availability of safe contraceptives; 3) changes in evidence required in rape cases, establishment of public shelters for women beaten by their husbands, establishment of self-defense classes; 4) equal credit opportunity, equal pay for equal work, equal pay for work of comparable value; and 5) equal legal treatment for lesbians and availability of contraception and abortion for minors (independent of parental consent).[16]

These more specific policy demands are not exclusively directed toward government for resolution. The various components of the feminist movement have relied upon a range of political strategies; hence the objects of those demands have included the mass media, universities, private corporations, and religious institutions, as well as legislatures, courts, and political parties, among others.

The ICPSR data for 1972 and 1976 permit some assessment of support for feminist issues, providing questions for both years concerning support for the women's liberation movement,[17] support for women's equality with men,[18] and support for abortion.[19] These variables have been used to form an additive index measuring support for feminist ideology.[20] Each of the variables in the index was recoded stringently,[21] because some of the questions asked have apparent "correct" answers in modern American society (such as support for women's equal political participation). Since a majority of Americans support the Equal Rights Amendment,[22] support for the amendment is not likely to separate feminists from non-feminists.

Our intention here is not a general examination of the impact of feminism upon participation but rather to set a consideration of feminism within the context of investigating unique sources of female participation. In this context, we are concerned primarily with understanding whether or not support for feminist issues has had a unique mobilizing effect upon women. It is possible—highly likely, in fact—that support for feminist issues may mobilize men to political action as well; but if that is the case, regardless of what else we may learn concerning feminism and participation, we will have to eliminate support for feminist issues as a source of political mobilization unique to women. And while it is possible—again, perhaps highly likely—that support for feminist issues may itself arise from different sources for women than for men,[23] the data which we employ herein cannot aid us in resolving that issue.

Since support for feminist issues is support for change, there is reason to believe that such support is related to political participation. Since the feminist movement emphasizes complete and equal involvement of women in the public as well as the private sphere, support for feminist issues should have a mobilizing effect upon women's participation, an effect which should not be evident for those who do not support such issues or for men. However, the feminist movement has been successful in achieving its demands from the political system by bringing unconventional political pressures to bear upon orthodox political institutions.[24] Therefore, we expect the following: 1) those who agree with feminist political issues will be more active politically than those who disagree (that is, we expect that the feminist movement has been successful in its aims of politically mobilizing women who support feminist issues); 2) feminists will be more active in all types of participation, in particular, in engaging in or approving of unconventional activism; and 3) women who support feminist issues will be more active than men who support them (in other words, we expect support for feminist issues to mobilize women for political participation, an impact that we do not expect it to have upon men).[25]

Table 22 shows the relationship between political participation and support for feminist issues, for activists with different levels of education. The table provides a range of support for feminist issues, from those most supportive (marked "1" on the table) to those least supportive (marked "4" on the table). With some exceptions, the data in this table suggest that there is a positive relationship between participation and support for feminist issues.

There are too few respondents with no high school experience[26] (marked "grade school" on the table) to draw any conclusions about the relationship between support for feminist issues and participation for these respondents. However, it is clear that among this group, most respondents do not support feminist issues. Among respondents with some high school education (marked "high school" on the table), there appears to be a slight relationship between support for feminist issues and some forms of participation. Support for feminist issues is related to political involvement and support for unconventional activism among high school educated women in 1972; support for feminist issues is likewise positively related to political involvement for both women and men by 1976. Support for feminist issues also increases feelings of political efficacy among women in 1972 and among female and male respondents in 1976, except for those who are "most feminist." For both women and men, feelings of political efficacy are slightly lower among respondents in this "most feminist" group than they are for the next most supportive group. However, other forms of political participation appear to be unrelated to support for feminist issues, for either women or men: voting, electoral and conventional activism (in 1972 and 1976), and unconventional activism in 1976.

The relationship between support for feminist issues and participation seems to be strongest among the college educated. Support for feminist issues is positively related to electoral and conventional activism (for 1972 and 1976) among college educated women and to support for unconventional participation for both sexes (1972). Political efficacy is likewise positively influenced by support for feminist issues, for women in 1972, and for both sexes by 1976. However, as with their high school educated counterparts, fewer college educated respondents who are most supportive of feminist issues report feelings of political efficacy, when compared with their less-supportive college educated peers (for 1976). Those who are most supportive of feminist issues, among both high school and college educated respondents, re-

Table 22.
Percent Active, and Total Number of, Women and Men, by Level of Education, 1972 and 1976

| | Grade School | | | | High School | | | | College | | | |
| | 1972 | | 1976 | | 1972 | | 1976 | | 1972 | | 1976 | |
	Women	Men	Women	Men	Women	Men	Women	Men	Women	Men	Women	Men
VOTING												
1.	*	80.0% (20)	*	87.5% (20)	72.5% (51)	66.7% (24)	65.2% (122)	65.7% (67)	91.4% (35)	*	82.1% (112)	80.0% (70)
2.	*	*	*	*	61.3 (62)	74.5 (47)	69.0 (84)	61.2 (52)	82.2 (45)	78.4 (37)	87.9 (50)	80.5 (64)
3.	62.2 (37)	76.2 (42)	*	*	84.0 (144)	74.3 (101)	54.1 (93)	59.6 (50)	89.9 (79)	85.0 (100)	84.7 (59)	82.4 (60)
4.	49.5 (99)	71.6 (74)	64.4 (82)	77.1 (66)	70.0 (333)	74.4 (176)	68.1 (349)	75.5 (178)	88.7 (106)	83.2 (125)	85.6 (136)	89.8 (128)
ELECTORAL ACTIVISM												
1.	*	10.0 (20)	*	*	15.7 (51)	20.8 (24)	7.9 (114)	16.7 (63)	48.6 (35)	*	30.5 (95)	24.4 (60)
2.	*	*	*	*	17.7 (62)	8.5 (47)	22.2 (79)	18.0 (45)	31.1 (45)	21.6 (37)	19.8 (48)	25.0 (50)
3.	2.7 (37)	16.7 (42)	*	*	14.2 (176)	18.0 (100)	10.9 (88)	9.8 (41)	30.4 (79)	27.0 (100)	24.2 (50)	16.5 (49)
4.	2.0 (99)	13.5 (74)	9.5 (79)	9.4 (64)	12.6 (334)	12.0 (175)	8.9 (319)	10.8 (167)	25.5 (106)	24.8 (125)	23.1 (128)	19.0 (116)

CONVENTIONAL ACTIVISM											
1.	*	0 (20)	*	5.0 (20)	7.8 (51)	16.7 (24)	7.0 (121)	4.5 (66)	22.9 (35)	*	17.7 (110)	26.4 (70)
2.	*	*	*	*	4.8 (62)	4.3 (47)	5.4 (83)	15.5 (52)	20.0 (45)	21.6 (37)	3.0 (50)	16.4 (64)
3.	2.7 (37)	2.4 (42)	*	*	5.7 (176)	10.9 (101)	5.4 (93)	3.1 (48)	13.9 (79)	11.0 (100)	9.5 (58)	5.0 (60)
4.	2.0 (99)	1.4 (74)	0 (79)	0 (66)	4.2 (334)	5.1 (176)	4.5 (344)	5.0 (177)	10.4 (106)	6.4 (125)	11.0 (136)	8.3 (128)
UNCONVENTIONAL ACTIVISM											
1.	*	*	*	0 (20)	12.0 (50)	4.2 (24)	0 (122)	0 (67)	40.0 (35)	*	4.5 (112)	7.9 (70)
2.	*	*	*	*	9.7 (62)	10.9 (46)	0 (84)	1.9 (52)	24.4 (45)	18.9 (37)	0 (50)	2.3 (64)
3.	0 (37)	0 (39)	*	*	4.1 (172)	6.0 (100)	0 (93)	0 (50)	7.6 (79)	15.3 (98)	4.2 (59)	2.6 (58)
4.	0 (87)	0 (73)	0 (80)	0 (66)	3.1 (327)	2.3 (171)	0.9 (349)	0 (177)	4.8 (105)	7.3 (124)	0 (136)	3.5 (128)

*N<20.

Note: Support for feminist issues ranges from (1) "most feminist" to (4) "least feminist."

107

Table 22 (*continued*)

| | Grade School | | | | High School | | | | College | | | |
| | 1972 | | 1976 | | 1972 | | 1976 | | 1972 | | 1976 | |
	Women	Men	Women	Men	Women	Men	Women	Men	Women	Men	Women	Men
POLITICAL INVOLVEMENT												
1.	*	*	*	*	30.4 (23)	*	22.0 (120)	28.4 (67)	*	*	41.6 (111)	41.4 (70)
2.	*	*	*	*	30.0 (20)	15.4 (26)	25.3 (83)	23.8 (51)	28.6 (28)	*	22.2 (50)	37.5 (64)
3.	*	21.7 (23)	*	*	25.3 (95)	32.0 (50)	16.8 (93)	13.1 (50)	31.4 (35)	43.8 (46)	34.7 (59)	30.3 (60)
4.	15.1 (53)	12.5 (40)	9.6 (79)	17.6 (66)	12.4 (170)	19.5 (87)	12.3 (345)	15.9 (174)	26.7 (60)	42.9 (63)	36.2 (136)	37.8 (127)
POLITICAL EFFICACY												
1.	*	*	*	30.0 (20)	21.6 (51)	16.7 (24)	16.7 (120)	29.9 (67)	48.6 (35)	*	35.3 (111)	51.4 (70)
2.	*	*	*	*	27.4 (62)	34.8 (46)	24.4 (84)	35.0 (52)	37.8 (45)	37.8 (37)	38.4 (50)	54.7 (64)
3.	10.8 (37)	19.5 (41)	*	*	22.3 (175)	28.7 (101)	19.5 (93)	35.4 (50)	31.6 (79)	43.9 (98)	34.7 (59)	49.6 (60)
4.	5.1 (99)	13.5 (74)	10.1 (80)	13.3 (64)	17.4 (333)	30.1 (176)	17.1 (345)	22.3 (178)	42.5 (106)	47.2 (125)	28.8 (130)	43.8 (128)

*N 20.

Note:

Support for feminist issues ranges from (1) "most feminist" to (4) "least feminist."

port slightly less political efficacy than their counterparts in the next most supportive group.

The positive relationship between support for feminist issues and political participation is more evident when we compare those who are most supportive of feminism with those who are least supportive. (Again, respondents with no high school education have been eliminated from consideration because there are too few of them.) Feminist supporters among the high school educated are most participant in eight of the twenty-four cases under consideration[27] (or a third of all cases), for both sexes. Feminist supporters among the college educated are most participant in eleven of the twenty-four cases[28] (or 45.8 percent of all cases). While support for feminist issues is more frequently related to participation among the college educated, it is related to participation among the high school educated as well.

Again, we argue that support for feminist issues ought to make more of a difference to women's political participation than it does to men's. Feminism, both as a political movement and as an ideology, addresses issues of unique importance to women, and the aim of the feminist movement has been to mobilize women for political action. Table 23 shows the participation differences between the "most feminist" women and men, by education, for 1972 and 1976. Comparisons of the impact of support for feminist issues upon women's and men's political participation indicate that feminism is related to participation for both, at least among those who are "most feminist." However, note that among the high school educated, for 1972, feminist women are more active than feminist men for three forms of participation (while feminist men are more active than their female counterparts in two cases), and that fewer than twenty men can be identified as "most feminist" among the politically involved. Note in addition, for 1972, that among the college educated, fewer than twenty men are identified as "most feminist" in all cases. In 1976, however, feminist men are as active as or more active than feminist women in all but one case—that of electoral activism.[29] The conclusion is, then, that while support for feminist issues has the same impact upon the political participation of both sexes, the differences between women and men were greater in the movement's early days, and that the movement had an important positive impact upon women's political participation, especially among the college educated.

Table 24 summarizes the uncontrolled relationship between support

Table 23.

Percent Active, and Total Number of, Feminist Women and Men, by Education, 1972 and 1976

	High School				College			
	1972		1976		1972		1976	
	Women	Men	Women	Men	Women	Men	Women	Men
Voting	72.5% (51)	66.7% (24)	65.2% (122)	65.7% (67)	91.4% (35)	*	82.1% (112)	8C.0% (70)
Electoral activism	15.7 (51)	20.8 (24)	7.9 (114)	16.7 (63)	48.6 (35)	*	30.5 (95)	24.4 (60)
Conventional activism	7.8 (51)	16.7 (24)	7.0 (121)	4.5 (66)	22.9 (35)	*	17.7 (110)	26.4 (70)
Unconventional activism[b]	12.0 (50)	4.2 (24)	0.0 (122)	0.0 (67)	40.0 (35)	*	4.5 (112)	7.9 (70)
Political involvement	30.4 (23)	*	22.0 (120)	28.4 (67)	*	*	41.6 (111)	41.4 (70)
Political efficacy	21.6 (51)	16.7 (24)	16.7 (120)	29.9 (67)	48.6 (35)	*	35.3 (111)	51.4 (70)

*N<20.

[a] Percentages report the participation of those who are ranked "most feminist"; see Table 22.

[b] The variable for 1972 measures support for such activity; the variable for 1976 measures actual unconventional participation.

for feminist issues and participation, for women and men for 1972 and 1976. Positive regression coefficients indicate a positive relationship between support for feminist issues and participation.[30]

The uncontrolled relationship between support for feminist issues and participation is stronger for both women and men in 1972 than it is in 1976. The relationship is stronger and statistically significant in all cases in 1972, although there is no evidence that propensity to vote is related to support—or lack of support—for feminist issues. By 1976, however, the pattern of the relationship between participation and support for feminist issues disappears. Support for feminist issues apparently had its impact upon women's political participation with the advent of the contemporary feminist movement; however, support for feminism is not the crucial variable. When the relationship is controlled for race, class, education, and age, the additional contribution of support for feminist issues to women's participation is greater than

Table 24.
The Uncontrolled Relationship between Support for Feminist Issues and Participation, Selected by Gender, 1972 and 1976

	1972		1976	
	Women	Men	Women	Men
Voting	.07	-.03	.02	-.06
Electoral activism	.16^c	.03	.10^a	.11^a
Conventional activism	.14^b	.16^b	.09^a	.08
Unconventional activism	.37^c	.15^b	.08^a	.06
Political involvement	.14^b	.05	.07	.15^c
Political efficacy	-.12^a	-.03	-.06	-.14^b

^{a} $p < .05.$ ^{b} $p < .01.$ ^{c} $p < .001.$

Note:
    Figures are standardized regression coefficients; when controlled for race, class, education, and age, support for feminist issues contributes less than 3 percent to the relationship, except for support for unconventional activism for both sexes for 1972 (10.7 percent for women, 4.4 percent for men), and for conventional activism among men in 1972 (3.9 percent). Negative coefficients for political efficacy indicate a positive relationship between support for feminist issues and efficacy.

3 percent in only one case—support for unconventional activism (the contribution for women is 10.7 percent). That is, support for feminist issues, at least in 1972, was very strongly related to other variables which have a positive impact upon political participation: race, class, age, and especially education.

CONCLUSION

The impact of the feminist movement upon women's political participation has been assessed in two ways in this chapter: first, as the movement's ability to develop a sense of group identity among women, and, second, as the movement's talents at developing women's support for major feminist issues, both general and specific. The latter measure is more strongly related to political participation, although each of these measures suggests some of the following about the relationship between feminism and political participation. First, the relationship between support for feminist issues and political participation varies according to education: the more educated the respondent, the more feminist and more participant. Second, the relationship between feminism and participation varies according to the type of participation: for example, voting is seemingly unrelated to feelings about feminism, while support for unconventional activism seems to be a component of support for feminism. Third, the relationship varies across the two data years: the relationship between feminism and women's political participation is strongest in 1972, a year when there was a great deal of feminist political activity and a time when the contemporary feminist movement was experiencing increasing strength, visibility, and support.[31] By 1976, however, the relationship becomes negligible.

Finally, the relationship between feminism and political participation is more similar for women and men than it is dissimilar. This is contrary to our claim that feminism—however measured—ought to have a unique impact upon women. "Feminist" men are more participant than non-feminist men, as is the case for women, and, by 1976, "feminist" men are occasionally more participant than feminist women. This suggests two possibilities, which are not necessarily exclusive. First, feminism may be simply a logical component of liberal ideology, a measure of support for "traditionally liberal" issues in general. "Support for feminist issues" explains more about participation for either women or men than does "feminist identification," suggesting that, by 1976, feminist issues such as support for the women's liberation movement, abortion, and an equal status for women were part of mainstream liberal ideology. In this sense, we should expect support for feminist issues to have similar effects upon the political participation of women and men.

Second, support for feminist issues is also highly related to level of education, regardless of gender. Again, in this case, we would expect support for feminist issues to be similarly related to political participation for men and women, education being an antecedent variable. In part, both of these possibilities support Andersen's suggestion that women's political participation has changed over time, in response both to feminism and education.[32] While feminism seems only weakly related to political participation by 1976, in 1972 it had a slightly, disproportionately positive impact upon women's political participation, especially among educated women, which it did not have upon men's. "Support for feminist issues,"then, suggests that the feminist

movement was successful in 1972 in linking support for feminist issues with the political mobilization of educated women.

NOTES

1. For a review of the contemporary feminist movement, see Jo Freeman,
The Politics of Women's Liberation (New York: David McKay, 1975); and
Sara Evans, *Personal Politics: The Roots of Women's Liberation in the Civil
Rights Movement and the New Left* (New York: Knopf, 1979).

2. For a discussion of the problems of creating group consciousness among
women, in contrast to other groups, see William Chafe, *Women and Equality:
Changing Patterns in American Culture* (New York: Oxford University Press,
1977), Chapter 1; and various essays in Patricia Caplan and Janet M. Bujra,
eds., *Women United, Women Divided* (Bloomington, Ind.: Indiana University
Press, 1980). See especially Bujra's introduction, "Female Solidarity and the
Sexual Division of Labor," pp. 13–45. See also Virginia Sapiro, *The Political Integration of Women* (Champaign, Ill.: University of Illinois Press, 1983),
for a discussion of "traditional" versus "nontraditional" women, pp. 73–75.

3. For a discussion of the political strategy of consciousness-raising, see
Kathie Sarachild, "Consciousness-Raising: A Radical Weapon," and Anne
Forer, "Thoughts on Consciousness-Raising," both in Redstockings, *Feminist
Revolution* (New York: Random House, 1978), pp. 144–151; and Carol Wil-
liams Payne, "Consciousness-Raising: A Dead End?," both in Ann Koedt,
Ellen Levine, and Anita Rapone, eds., *Radical Feminism* (New York: Quad-
rangle, 1973), pp. 280–284.

4. See, for example, Richard D. Shingles, "Black Consciousness and
Political Participation: The Missing Link," *American Political Science Review*, LXXV (1), March 1981, pp. 76–91.

5. Sidney Verba and Norman Nie, *Participation in America: Political
Democracy and Social Equality* (New York: Harper and Row, 1972), p. 161.

6. Arthur H. Miller, et al., "Group Consciousness and Political Participation," *American Journal of Political Science*, XXV (3), August 1981, p. 508.
They define "group consciousness" as a combination of four components: 1)
group identification, 2) polar affect, 3) polar power, and 4) individual versus
system blame. See Ibid., pp. 496–497.

7. Ibid., p. 509.

8. The 1976 question reads:

We'd also like to get your feelings about some groups in American society. When I
read the name of a group, we'd like you to rate it with what we call a feeling thermometer. Ratings between 50 and 100 degrees mean that you feel favorably and warmly
toward the group; ratings between 0 and 50 degrees mean that you don't feel favorably

toward the group and that you don't care too much for that group. If you don't feel particularly warm or cold toward a group, you would rate them at 50 degrees. If we come to a group you don't know much about, just tell me and we'll move on to the next one. . . . Women's liberation movement?

See *American National Election Studies*, vol. I, Introduction and Codebook (Ann Arbor: ICPSR, 1976), pp. 419 and 425.

9. For a different approach to the issue of female and male feminist sympathizers, see Ethel Klein, *Gender Politics* (Cambridge, Mass.: Harvard University Press, 1984), Chapters Seven and Eight.

10. The 1972 unconventional activism index measures support for protest activities; the 1976 unconventional activism index measures actual participation.

11. While there is some evidence that, among college educated women, feminist group identification is related to political participation, the data do not allow us to claim with certainty that feminist group identification is the source—rather than the result—of such participation. It may well be that women who have been active as the result of other factors (e.g., age, class) have come to identify with the feminist movement as a result of their activism. However, an examination of the changes in differences in participation between female feminist identifiers and nonidentifiers, between 1972 and 1976, suggests that this is not the case. Instead of what we might expect if feminist identification were the result rather than the source of activism (an increase in differences in participation between feminist identifiers and nonidentifiers from 1972 to 1976), we find instead no increase or decrease in differences. If activism were the source of feminist group identification, if activism served as some form of consciousness-raising for women, then the data ought to demonstrate an increase in the differences between activist feminist identifiers and nonidentifiers between 1972 and 1976. The data do not demonstrate this.

12. The "feminist group identity" variables were not recoded for Table 21. Hence, feminist group identity for 1972 is measured as support for women's liberation, on a seven-point scale where "1" represents no support and "7" represents strong approval. For 1976, feminist group identity is measured on a "feeling thermometer," where "0" represents very unfavorable feelings and "99" represents extremely favorable feelings toward the women's liberation movement.

13. In 1972, for women, controlling for education, race, class, and age, feminist group identification made a 9.4 percent difference in unconventional participation, in the expected direction.

14. For an analysis of the relationship between the liberal and the radical components of the contemporary feminist movement, see Zillah Eisenstein, *The Radical Future of Liberal Feminism* (New York: Longman, 1981); and Carol Hanish, "The Liberal Takeover of Women's Liberation," in Redstockings, *Feminist Revolution*. Despite the differences between the bourgeois (or

liberal) and radical branches of the feminist movement, there has been an increasing agreement in recent years on several issues previously rejected by the liberal branch—the best example of which is the National Organization for Women's (NOW) advocacy of lesbian rights.

15. For a statement of the goals and issues of the radical wing of the contemporary feminist movement, see Kate Millet, "Sexual Politics: A Manifesto for Revolution," "The Feminists: A Political Organization to Annihilate Sex Roles," "Politics of the Ego: A Manifesto for New York Radical Feminists," "Westchester Radical Feminists," and Joreen, "The Bitch Manifesto," all in Koedt et al., *Radical Feminism*; Maryanne Weathers, "An Argument for Black Women's Liberation as a Revolutionary Force," Alix Shulman, "A Marriage Agreement," Rosalyn Baxandall, "Cooperative Nurseries," and Sookie Stambler, "Introduction," all in Sookie Stambler, ed., *Women's Liberation: A Blueprint for the Future* (New York: Ace Books, 1970); "Redstockings Manifesto," "Southern Female Rights Union Program for Female Liberation," "Lillith's Manifesto," "Congress to Unite Women—What Women Want," "Women Unite for Revolution," Vicki Pollard, "Producing Society's Babies," Louise Gross and Phyllis MacEwan, "On Day Care," Carol Driscoll, "The Abortion Problem," Betsy Warrior, "Sex Roles and Their Consequences," Barbara Balogun (Jackson), "Marriage as an Oppressive Institution/Collectives as Solutions," Pat Mainardi, "The Politics of Housework," and "Analyses of the Movement," by various authors, in Leslie B. Tanner, ed., *Voices From Women's Liberation* (New York: Mentor, 1970); Kathy McAfee and Myrna Wood, "Bread and Roses," and Barbara Burris et al., "Fourth World Manifesto," in Roberta Salper, ed., *Female Liberation* (New York: Knopf, 1972); Ti-Grace Atkinson, various essays in *Amazon Odyssey* (New York: Links, 1974).

The goals and perspectives of the "mainstream" branch of the movement, often referred to as "bourgeois feminism," can be found in Lisa Hammel, "NOW Organized," Aileen Hernandez, "Editorial from NOW's President," and Alice Rossi, "Equality Between the Sexes: An Immodest Proposal" and "Visions of the Future," in June Sochen, ed., *The New Feminisms in Twentieth-Century America* (Lexington, Mass.: D. C. Heath, 1971); Betty Friedan, "Our Revolution Is Unique," Alice Rossi, "Sex Equality: The Beginnings of an Ideology," and Caroline Bird, "The Androgenous Life," in Mary Lou Thompson, ed., *Voices of the New Feminism* (Boston: Beacon, 1970); Freeman, *The Politics of Women's Liberation*, Chapters 2 and 3; Betty Friedan, *The Feminine Mystique* (New York: Dell, 1964); and Caroline Bird, *Born Female* (New York: McKay, 1974).

16. Good sources of specific policy proposals of the feminist movement are *The NOW Times*, the weekly official publication of NOW; *Ms.* magazine, for the liberal feminist perspective; and *off our backs*, an autonomous monthly feminist newspaper, for the radical-lesbian perspective.

17. This variable is measured by a seven-point scale, ranging from strong disapproval of women's liberation to strong approval of women's liberation (for 1972), and by a "feeling thermometer" ranging from "0" or cold feelings for the women's liberation movement to "99" or warm feelings for the women's liberation movement (1976). The 1976 feeling thermometer was recoded so that a score of 85 or above represented support for women's liberation and scores below 85 represented a lack of support for women's liberation; the 1972 seven-point scale was recoded so that a score of seven (or strong support) represented support for women's liberation and a score of six or less indicated lack of support. See the 1972 and 1976 *American National Elections Studies*, Volumes II and I.

18. This question, for 1972 and 1976, reads: "Recently there has been a lot of talk about women's rights. Some people feel that women should have an equal role with men in running business, industry, and government. Others feel that women's place is in the home. Where would you place yourself on this scale, or haven't you thought much about this?", where "1" represents "women and men should have an equal role" and where "7" represents "women's place is in the home." The distribution of responses to this question is as follows:

726	1.	Women and men should have an equal role.
277	2.	
198	3.	
427	4.	
179	5.	
111	6.	
251	7.	Women's place is in the home.

Of a total of 2,872 respondents, 703 did not answer this question. Note that 33.5 percent of all those who answered the question gave the most equalitarian response; over half the respondents (55.4 percent) gave a reply above the midpoint "4" of this scale. This variable has been recoded so that responses ranging from "2" to "7" represent a lack of support for women's equality. See the 1976 *American National Election Study*, Volume I, p. 406.

19. This question, for 1972 and 1976, reads: "Still on the subject of women's rights, there has been some discussion about abortion during recent years. Which one of the opinions on this page best agrees with your view?" The range of choices listed is:

1. Abortion should never be permitted.
2. Abortion should be permitted only if the life and health of the woman are in danger.
3. Abortion should be permitted if, due to personal reasons, the woman would have difficulty in caring for the child.
4. Abortion should never be forbidden, since one should not require a woman to have a child she doesn't want.

The distribution of responses to the question is: 1) 11.1 percent (254); 2) 45.4 percent (1,041); 3) 16.5 percent (379); and 4) 27.0 percent (619). The total for those who gave some other response is 579. This question was recoded so that the fourth response, no prohibitions against abortion, represented support for abortion and all other responses indicated lack of support for abortion.

20. This index was formed by simply standardizing the individual variables and then summing the standardized scores.

21. See fns. 15, 16, and 17 for specific explanation of recoding.

22. The question of support for the Equal Rights Amendment, available only for 1976 in the ICPSR data, shows that 1,665 respondents (or 81.1 percent) approved of the amendment, 388 (or 18.9 percent) disapproved, and 817 did not respond. See the 1976 *American National Election Study*, Volume I, p. 409. In contrast, however, see Janet K. Boles, *The Politics of the Equal Rights Amendment* (New York: Longman, 1979), p. 102, for 1976 Gallup poll data on support for the amendment; 57 percent favored the amendment, 24 percent opposed it, and 19 percent had no opinion. See also Mary Fainsod Katzenstein, "Feminism and the Meaning of the Vote," *Signs*, X (1), 1984, pp. 4–26; and Mark R. Daniels, Robert Darcy, and Joseph W. Westphal, "The ERA Won—At Least in the Opinion Polls," *PS*, 15 (4), Fall 1982, pp. 578–584.

23. See Klein, *Gender Politics*, Chapters Seven and Eight.

24. Some of the more unconventional political tactics used by the feminist movement have included the WITCH (Women's International Terrorist Conspiracy from Hell) curse on Wall Street in 1968, which "caused" the market to drop; the 1968 protest demonstration in Atlantic City during the Miss America Pageant, to draw attention to the sexist premium placed on women's physical appearance; petitions in support of legalized abortion, in the late 1960s and early 1970s, signed only by women who had obtained illegal abortions. Frances Fox Piven and Richard Cloward, *Poor People's Movements* (New York: Vintage, 1979), discuss the success that political movements can have using unorthodox forms of political participation, which they refer to as "direct action." See their Introduction and Chapter I, especially.

25. Knoche examined the possibility that adherence to feminism may be *negatively* related to political participation, insofar as feminism represents an anti-system ideology, and that feminism is more likely to be related to feelings of political alienation, cynicism, and hostility to the political system, and hence to low levels of participation (Claire Fulenwider Knoche, "Political Ramifications of Feminism: A Quantitative Analysis of Participation and Alienation," paper presented at the 1977 meetings of the American Political Science Association, Washington, D.C.). Knoche defined political alienation as a combination of high unconventional activism and low feelings of political efficacy; however, she found no such combination in her work. Therefore, we

have no reason to expect that support for feminist issues, as measured here, should be associated with noticeably lower levels of participation, since the components of the feminist issues index are more likely representative of change-oriented aspects of feminism than any antisystem feelings which might result in less participation. Nor is there any reason to assume that antisystem feelings would not result in additional political mobilization among women who support feminist issues.

26. Level of education has been recoded for presentation of percentage distributions. "Grade school" refers to those whose maximum education is the completion of elementary school (up to and including eighth grade). "High school" refers to those who have had some high school education, up to and including a high school diploma. "College" refers to those who have had some college education, up to and including a college degree. Those who have had additional education, of whom there are very few in the 1972 and 1976 samples, have been excluded from consideration.

27. Among high school educated women, those who are most supportive of feminist issues are at least 5 percent more participant than their sisters who are least supportive of such issues, in the following cases: unconventional activism, involvement, and political efficacy in 1972, and political involvement in 1976. Among high school educated men, those who are most supportive of feminist issues are at least 5 percent more participant than their brothers who are least supportive of such issues, in the following cases: electoral and conventional activism in 1972; electoral participation, involvement, and political efficacy in 1976.

28. Among college educated women, those who are most supportive of feminist issues are at least 5 percent more active than their counterparts who are least supportive of those issues, in these cases: electoral activism, conventional and unconventional participation, and political efficacy in 1972, and electoral activism, conventional participation, political involvement, and political efficacy in 1976.

Among college educated men, those who are most supportive of feminist issues are at least 5 percent more active than their counterparts who are least supportive of those issues, in these cases: electoral, conventional, and unconventional participation, and political efficacy in 1976. There were fewer than twenty men, among the college educated, in 1972, who were most supportive of feminism.

29. Women who are most supportive of feminist issues are at least 5 percent more active than their male counterparts in the following cases: among high school educated women, in the cases of voting, unconventional activism, and political efficacy in 1972; and among college educated women, in the case of electoral activism in 1976. Note that, among college educated male respondents, in 1972, fewer than twenty could be identified as being most supportive of feminist issues.

30. For political efficacy, however, a positive regression coefficient indicates agreement with the statement that ''sometimes politics and government seem too complicated for a person like me to understand.'' Hence, a negative regression coefficient indicates a positive relationship between support for feminist issues and sense of political efficacy.

31. For example, the Equal Rights Amendment to the Constitution was proposed by Congress in 1972.

32. Andersen, ''Working Women.'' Note that Andersen's study ends with 1972 data.

—————————————————————

CHAPTER VI

WOMEN'S POLITICAL PARTICIPATION: ALTERNATIVE CONSIDERATIONS OF CLASS AND RACE

Women's work outside and inside the home, feminism, and the experience of women in political generations are all variables that were expected to have a special impact upon women's political participation—an impact unique to women. In general, these variables have been shown to influence not only women's participation, but men's political participation as well. Other variables—which political scientists have long demonstrated are related to political participation—have not been discussed: for examples, social class and race. While childcare, for example, is experienced differently by women and men in the United States, it seems to have the same general effect upon women's and men's political participation. Race and social class are also experienced differently by women and men, although race and social class may have similar importance as "political facts" for women and men. Therefore, this chapter will briefly review the literature about the different ways that race and social class are experienced and understood by boys and girls. Second, the impact of these different experiences of similar circumstances upon political participation will be examined. Finally, the difference between these variables and those which were thought to be unique to women will be considered, and some conclusions drawn.

SOCIAL CLASS BACKGROUND

The difference among classes in socializing children is not readily apparent. There is little information concerning the signals daughters of the working class receive in contrast to those received by middle-class girls, aside from the hint that neither will be considered as politically important as her brother.[1] However, there is some indirectly related information that suggests that working-class girls are not socialized to an active political gender role, while their middle- and upper-class counterparts are. This class differentiated socialization is more than simply the difference between how working- and middle-class *children* are socialized, but the different gender-role socialization that *girls* of each class receive.

The major arguments concerning gender-role socialization differences by class are that gender roles are more clearly defined and differentiated in the working class than in the middle class and that the working class is more patriarchal.[2] S. M. Miller and Frank Riessman argue that some of the "essential characteristics of the stable American worker today" are that "he [*sic*] is traditional, 'old-fashioned,' somewhat religious, and patriarchal."[3] Donald McKinley finds that among the lower classes, "one of the more universal aspects of authoritarianism is the tendency toward rigid dichotomization of male and female sex roles."[4] He continues: "Sex groups are *the* significant reference groups for the individual in defining what he should and should not do, what his aspirations are, and how he should relate to people."[5]

Helen Mayer Hacker supports this finding:

The differences in the upbringing of working-class boys and girls lead to social distance. Not only are girls early absorbed as mother's helpers and boys dissuaded from any interests or activities labeled feminine, but both sexes come to rely on same-sex gangs and cliques for friendship, moral support, and validations of self-worth.[6]

Lee Rainwater, Richard Coleman, and Gerald Handel observe that gender roles in the working class, while not necessarily hierarchical, are separate and distinct;[7] Paul Blumberg summarizes:

There is . . . relatively little sharing and cooperation between husband and wife of childcare and housework; each has his [*sic*] responsibilities. . . . As a result of her tremendous household responsibilities, her isolation from the world of clubs, her limited education and sparse intellectual resources, her early marriage and motherhood, the working-class wife lives a very sheltered existence, completely cut off from the larger world outside.[8]

Finally, Hacker concludes that in families "nominally headed by the least educated, least mobile blue-collar husbands and fathers, a clear segregation of gender roles obtains. . . . Both sexes subscribe to an ideology of patriarchy and male dominance."[9]

The agreement among authors that lower- and working-class families are more likely to demonstrate rigid role differences than are middle- and upper-class families, with the male role oriented to the work world and the female role oriented to the home and family, leads to the conclusion that daughters of working-class parents are less likely to have been socialized to an active political role than are their brothers and their counterparts from the middle class.

Participation Differences between Women: Class Background

Tables 25 and 26 show the differences in participation among four groups of people, for two levels of education: women and men of middle-class family background and women and men of working-class family background,[10] for those who have some high school education and for those who have some college education. For both women and men, with similar class backgrounds, those who have some college education are more active than those who do not. For those with similar educational attainment, however, those from middle-class families are not always more active than those from working-class families, nor do controls for educational attainment and class background eliminate gender related differences in participation.

First, middle-class women with college educations are not consistently more active, involved, or efficacious than their sisters from the working class (see Table 25). There are few differences in voting, for example, between college educated women of different class backgrounds, and there are no differences in unconventional activism (although women from the middle class are slightly more supportive of such activity). Women from middle-class families are more conventionally active (about 10 percent) than their working-class counterparts until 1976, when the differences disappear. Middle-class women with college educations are generally more involved than working-class women, but the percentage differences fluctuate across years. The most unusual pattern for this group of college educated women is that until 1968, women from the working class report higher levels of efficacy

Table 25.
Percent Active, and Total Number of, Respondents, by Gender and Social Class Background: College Educated

	1956 Women	1956 Men	1960 Women	1960 Men	1964 Women	1964 Men	1968 Women	1968 Men	1976 Women	1976 Men
VOTING										
middle-class	88.2% (102)	89.5% (95)	84.4% (77)	93.8% (48)	87.9% (99)	86.1% (79)	80.4% (107)	86.5% (74)	84.7% (225)	81.0% (142)
working-class	87.5 (48)	94.7 (76)	85.7 (42)	90.7 (43)	93.2 (44)	90.4 (73)	75.0 (64)	84.0 (81)	81.6 (152)	87.5 (185)
ELECTORAL PARTICIPATION										
middle-class	25.5 (102)	24.2 (95)	34.2 (73)	29.8 (47)	30.6 (98)	30.4 (79)	27.7 (101)	24.6 (69)	27.5 (200)	11.2 (123)
working-class	27.1 (48)	27.0 (74)	25.6 (39)	20.0 (40)	20.5 (44)	31.9 (72)	14.8 (61)	28.6 (77)	17.8 (138)	20.6 (156)
CONVENTIONAL PARTICIPATION										
middle-class	**	**	**	**	35.4 (99)	34.2 (79)	39.9 (103)	35.7 (70)	40.8 (224)	46.5 (142)
working-class	**	**	**	**	27.3 (44)	28.9 (73)	30.2 (63)	38.5 (78)	42.8 (152)	42.5 (185)

UNCONVENTIONAL PARTICIPATION[a]										
middle-class	**	**	**	**	**	**	26.0 (96)	33.9 (68)	2.0 (250)	3.7 (161)
working-class	**	**	**	**	**	**	20.0 (55)	14.4 (76)	2.2 (186)	3.4 (209)
POLITICAL INVOLVEMENT										
middle-class	32.0 (100)	25.8 (93)	50.0 (72)	62.5 (48)	48.5 (97)	46.2 (78)	38.2 (102)	33.3 (69)	40.0 (224)	37.0 (142)
working-class	30.4 (46)	32.0 (75)	35.3 (34)	38.5 (39)	41.9 (43)	41.7 (72)	34.4 (61)	39.5 (76)	26.6 (152)	38.1 (184)
POLITICAL EFFICACY										
middle-class	52.0 (100)	68.4 (95)	46.1 (76)	77.1 (48)	48.6 (107)	72.9 (85)	66.1 (112)	79.2 (77)	35.9 (220)	45.1 (142)
working-class	68.8 (48)	69.7 (76)	64.3 (42)	67.4 (43)	54.9 (51)	48.7 (78)	66.7 (63)	79.1 (91)	27.8 (150)	49.0 (184)

**No data are available for these variables for these years. Note as well that information about social class background is unavailable for 1952 and 1972.

[a]Note that this variable measures support for unconventional activism in 1968, and actual unconventional participation in 1976.

Table 26.
Percent Active, and Total Number of, Respondents, by Gender and Social Class Background: High School Educated

	1956 Women	1956 Men	1960 Women	1960 Men	1964 Women	1964 Men	1968 Women	1968 Men	1976 Women	1976 Men
VOTING										
middle-class	76.1% (155)	85.1% (101)	87.3% (79)	89.8% (59)	79.3% (135)	89.6% (77)	80.7% (119)	83.3% (54)	66.5% (237)	64.9% (87)
working-class	67.9 (361)	78.3 (240)	71.2 (316)	80.8 (266)	74.1 (313)	77.1 (201)	76.9 (286)	76.5 (187)	63.5 (516)	71.4 (318)
ELECTORAL PARTICIPATION										
middle-class	21.4 (154)	20.8 (101)	23.0 (74)	25.5 (55)	17.8 (135)	16.2 (74)	15.3 (111)	8.0 (50)	9.6 (219)	12.1 (87)
working-class	7.8 (361)	14.6 (240)	13.1 (290)	15.3 (249)	12.3 (309)	13.0 (200)	14.3 (272)	13.6 (177)	9.9 (480)	10.6 (288)
CONVENTIONAL PARTICIPATION										
middle-class	**	**	**	**	19.3 (135)	10.4 (77)	16.8 (133)	13.5 (52)	24.8 (232)	33.9 (87)
working-class	**	**	**	**	13.1 (312)	16.9 (201)	14.0 (278)	19.6 (179)	22.4 (513)	26.4 (315)

UNCONVENTIONAL PARTICIPATION[a]									
middle-class	**	**	**	**	**	**	13.1 (99)	8.5 (47)	0.6 (266)	0.0 (115)
working-class	**	**	**	**	**	**	11.6 (232)	10.0 (161)	0.2 (612)	0.3 (396)
POLITICAL INVOLVEMENT										
middle-class	23.4 (154)	25.7 (101)	50.0 (74)	56.4 (55)	28.9 (135)	39.0 (77)	19.6 (112)	29.4 (51)	18.0 (233)	23.4 (86)
working-class	8.4 (358)	12.7 (236)	31.0 (284)	40.4 (240)	13.5 (310)	15.7 (197)	16.5 (273)	15.6 (179)	14.9 (513)	17.2 (315)
POLITICAL EFFICACY										
middle-class	40.9 (154)	53.5 (101)	50.0 (78)	56.5 (58)	28.9 (142)	41.5 (82)	56.1 (132)	71.7 (60)	19.4 (232)	30.5 (87)
working-class	29.1 (357)	37.8 (238)	32.2 (311)	44.5 (263)	22.0 (323)	34.6 (211)	49.0 (314)	58.7 (206)	17.2 (506)	25.2 (316)

**No data are available for these variables for these years. Note as well that information about social class background is unavailable for 1952 and 1972.

[a]Note that this variable measures support for unconventional activism in 1968, and actual unconventional participation in 1976.

than women from the middle class. By 1968, these differences disappear, and the relationship is reversed by 1976. Nonetheless, we might suggest that these higher percentages of reported efficacy have a material basis, at least for these early years, in that women from working-class backgrounds have achieved a great deal—given the restraints society places upon them because of the combination of their gender and class background—by obtaining higher education and that personal achievement is the source of their positive feelings about potential political achievement.

The case is somewhat different for high school educated women of different class backgrounds (see Table 26). The general pattern over time is that women from the middle class are more active, involved, and efficacious than are their working-class counterparts. For voting, electoral activism, conventional participation, involvement, and political efficacy, women from the working class participate less.[11] However, the relatively large percentage differences found in the early years diminish across time, so that by 1976 class background is seemingly unrelated to any form of political participation.

The suggestion that daughters of working-class parents are less likely to have been socialized to an active political role than their middle-class counterparts is not completely borne out by the data.[12] Although working-class women are generally less participant than middle-class women, much of that participation difference can be explained by differences in education, rather than social class background itself. We should be cautious, however, about concluding that social class background makes relatively little difference for women's political participation. First, for women, the effects of class differences (and related socialization differences) are not completely eliminated when education is controlled. Participation among working-class and middle-class daughters is most similar among the college educated, but class differences are still evident among the high school educated.

Second, while education is positively related to political participation, social class background is also related to education. Women from working-class families have lower levels of educational attainment than men or than women from the middle class. If working-class girls are not encouraged to seek higher education—or if they are prohibited from doing so—then the positive relationship between education and participation is, in a sense, irrelevant. If few working-class girls become well educated, and, as a result, are less active, we can hardly conclude that social class is not an important factor. On the contrary, social class background becomes an important antecedent variable.

Gender Related Differences in Participation: Class Background

Again, controls for education and social class background do not eliminate gender related differences in participation. In general, men report being more active, involved, and efficacious than women, regardless of class background and educational attainment. However, gender related participation differences appear to be greatest among those of working-class background and among those with less than a college education (see again Tables 25 and 26).

Among the college educated, there are few gender related differences in voting, in electoral and conventional participation, and in political involvement, for those of middle-class family background.[13] Middle-class men are more supportive of unconventional activism than are their sisters (1968), but both women and men of middle-class background are unconventionally inactive (1976). The largest gender related difference for this group is in feelings of political efficacy. College educated women of middle-class background report much less political efficacy than do their male counterparts. Percentage differences between these two groups are 16.4 percent in 1956, 31.0 percent in 1960, 24.3 percent in 1964, 13.1 percent in 1968, and 9.2 percent in 1976. While differences between college educated middle-class women and men have been diminishing across time, a substantial difference in reported feelings of political efficacy still remains in 1976. Comparable differences in involvement and participation, however, are not evident.

For those from working-class backgrounds, with some college education, gender related differences are more apparent but have been diminishing over time. Except for 1964, there is at least a 5 percent difference in voting turnout between men and women in this group. There are some gender related differences in electoral participation for this group: men are more active in 1964 and 1968 (11.4 and 13.8 percentage differences, respectively), although men's and women's electoral participation is roughly similar for other years. However, college educated women and men participate at similar rates in conventional and unconventional activism and (until 1976) demonstrate the

same levels of political involvement.[14] The pattern for political efficacy, however, is unclear. Women and men in this group report similar feelings of political efficacy in the early years, but by 1964 the
women in this category report more efficacy than their male counterparts. By 1968 and 1976, however, the pattern has reversed, with men
in this category appearing more efficacious. In these two recent years
of study, the pattern for those of working-class background is more
similar to that for those of middle-class background (12.4 percentage
difference in 1968 and 21.2 percentage difference by 1976).

For the high school educated, we might expect that gender related
participation differences would be greatest, especially for those of
working-class background. The data in Table 26 show that this is not
the case. For those of middle-class background with high school educations, there are few gender related differences in voting participation, electoral activism, unconventional activism (1976), and support
for unconventional participation (1968). Middle-class women with high
school educations, however, are more conventionally active than their
male counterparts (at least until 1976) but slightly less politically involved. They also feel less politically efficacious. Gender related differences in political involvement, for those of middle-class background with some high school education, increase slightly from 1956
to 1964 and decrease somewhat thereafter. Male-female percentage
differences are 2.3 percent in 1956, 6.4 percent in 1960, 10.1 percent
in 1964, 9.8 percent in 1968, and 5.4 percent in 1976. Gender related
efficacy differences, however, remain constant. Percentage differences
in political efficacy, for men and women of this same group, are 12.6
percent in 1956, 8.6 percent in 1960, 12.6 percent in 1964, 15.6 percent in 1968, and 11.1 percent in 1976.

An examination of the relationship between participation and gender
for those of working-class background with some high school education shows the following. Being from the working class has approxi-
mately the same impact upon participation for women and men as it
does for those of the middle class, when education is held constant.
Working-class women vote less than do their brothers, but gender related differences in voting disappear during the 1960s. Women and
men of working-class background participate similarly in electoral,
conventional, and unconventional activities and show similar levels of
support (or lack thereof) for unconventional participation by others.
These women and men also report similar levels of political involve-

ment across time, with the largest difference (9.4 percent) occurring in 1960. Despite this, however, working-class women report less political efficacy than their male counterparts. This difference persists across time and is fairly constant in magnitude. Percentage differences in efficacy are 8.7 percent in 1956, 12.3 percent in 1960, 12.6 percent in 1964, 9.7 percent in 1968, and 8.0 percent in 1976.

We suggested earlier in this chapter that daughters of working-class parents are less likely than their brothers or than their middle-class counterparts to have been socialized to an active political role. That claim cannot be substantiated or refuted by these data, but the evidence can suggest how patterns of participation among women and men of different classes might reflect differences in socialization. We expected that: 1) working-class women, regardless of education, would be somewhat less likely than middle-class women to participate in politics and 2) that working-class women, regardless of education, would also be less likely than their brothers to participate in politics. While the evidence is not definitive, it does suggest that only the first of these claims is correct. Although there are exceptions, women of working-class background are somewhat less active than their middle-class sisters. This is most evident, however, among women with high school educations and much less evident among college educated women. Working-class women are also less likely to participate in politics than are their middle-class brothers. However, the average percentage difference in participation between working-class women and men is no greater than the average percentage difference in participation between women and men from the middle class. Therefore, these participation differences may reflect a general socialization away from politics, which little girls experience, regardless of class—rather than a gender-role socialization unique to the working class.[15]

RACE

The literature on political socialization of girls finds evidence of race related differences in socialization, with black girls being socialized to a more independent, achievement oriented role than white girls. This difference in socialization reflects the different social, economic, and political conditions faced by the races in the United States and, for black girls, the historical role of "perverted equality" which has been thrust upon black women since slavery.[16] Virginia O'Leary argues that: "those characteristics . . . most valued in Black women within the Black community [include] strength, independence, and resourcefulness." [17]

O'Leary documents her assertion with evidence from a variety of studies of gender-role beliefs among black and white children and adults, which show that blacks endorse fewer gender-role differences than whites and are less likely to endorse masculine-feminine differences. [18] Black women are less likely to "fear success" than white women (even when class differences are controlled), because "Black women do not perceive competitively-based achievement as incompatible with their concept of femininity." [19] O'Leary cites Ladner's study that shows that

the most prevalent conception of womanhood that existed among the preadult [black] females interviewed . . . was that of strength and resourcefulness. . . . Thus, their conception of femininity focused on the ability to accept responsibility, and the traits they valued most highly in women were strength, resourcefulness, and self-reliance. [20]

Conceptions of white femininity were more frequently evidenced among black girls of upper-income families than among girls from middle-and lower-class families. O'Leary concludes by arguing that "sex role stereotypes appear to be less well differentiated in the Black community than within the broader culture." [21] O'Leary argues that the roles for black girls are more flexible and diffused than the roles white girls envision for themselves. Gender-role identification may or may not be as strong, but the gender role for black girls and women seems to permit greater independence, self-reliance, and achievement.

The gender roles outlined by O'Leary and others for black girls and women would be likely to encourage an active, autonomous participation of black women in politics. O'Leary suggests that the black church and the black community have been traditional forums for black female political participation, but that the rise of a male-dominated Black Liberation movement in the late 1960s may have served to undermine some of that traditional sphere for participation. [22] In sum, the gender-role socialization of black girls and women suggests that they cannot be treated in the same way in the study of women's political participation as are white women. [23]

The question of race differences in women's political participation is complicated by racism in America. The experience of black women under slavery and within the black community includes poverty and race discrimination, which discourage political participation.[24] Therefore, a strong self-image among black women, particularly those of lower-income groups, should support political participation, but their lower levels of education and income should predict lower levels of participation.

John Pierce and others argue that impoverished black women have relatively—and given their situations, surprisingly—high levels of political participation.[25] Therefore, the traditional assumptions concerning income, class, and education and political participation have to be held in abeyance during an examination of the separate and peculiar relationships between black women's socialization and political participation. While less-educated, lower-class white women may be among those citizens least likely to participate in politics, their black counterparts may be among the most likely citizens to participate in politics, although the forms and purposes of that participation may be very different.

It would be impossible within the confines of this study to examine all the reasons for the political behavioral differences between white and black women; the differences themselves are not completely known and the reasons for the differences are clouded by the controversies surrounding previous "scholarship" on black women.[26] Again, the problems of addressing sources of discrimination for racial differences are similar to those of gender related differences. The contribution of each in influencing women's political participation cannot be assessed in this study.

There is an additional problem in examining the case of black women. This is the problem of small numbers.[27] For each year under study, the total number of black women rarely exceeds one hundred. Therefore, it is difficult to break down these numbers into smaller cells to control for class, education, and income differences and other relevant variables. The following, however, is a brief examination of the participation differences between women according to race, controlled for education.

Race Related Differences in Women's Participation

A major difficulty in comparing the patterns of participation of white and black women is that, again, there are so few black people in the survey samples and, consequently, fewer black women. When race related differences in participation are controlled for education, the numbers of black women per cell become very small—so small that there are not enough college educated blacks in the samples to permit comparison of behavior with whites. The following tables present information about the political participation of men and women of different races for only two levels of educational attainment: grade school and high school. Note that even for those with a high school education, for most years there are so few black men that male-female comparisons become impossible. Given that educational attainment is and has been historically related to race, however, race, like social class background, becomes an important antecedent variable in the relationship between education and participation.

In general, participation differences between white and black *women with only grade school educations* are small (see Table 27).

Levels of electoral participation, political involvement, and political efficacy are relatively low for women of each race, and, as a result, racial differences in participation are minimal. Only for two types of participation do white women show more activism: voting and conventional behavior. In the case of voting, racial differences are dramatically large, but steadily decreasing, from the 1950s until the 1968 election, when the voting participation rates of each group of women become similar. These diminishing differences in turnout are surely in response to changes in electoral law which made voting participation accessible to blacks. In the case of conventional behavior, the differences are not dramatic, but they are constant: 7.1 percent in 1964, 5.5 percent in 1968, 7.6 percent in 1972, and 9.4 percent in 1976. Since conventional political participation is similar to what Verba and Nie refer to as "parochial participation," it is less than surprising to find some race related difference here.[28]

There are two types of participation, however, where black women report more activism than do white women: unconventional activism and political efficacy. Black women with grade school educations report much higher support for unconventional activism (1968, 1972) than do their white counterparts, although both black and white women are similarly inactive unconventionally (1976). Since blacks in general are disproportionately represented among those who engage in unconventional activity,[29] it is not surprising that black women would show

higher levels of approval than white women for this kind of participation.

Political efficacy differences are inconsistent and vary from year to
year with little apparent pattern.[30] Efficacy levels of black women are
similar to those of white women, except for 1960, 1968, and 1976,
when efficacy levels of black women are higher than those of white
women. While black women's feelings of efficacy may be tied to these
years because of the specific presidential elections, it is not clear that
this is so. However, 1960, 1968, and 1976 were all years when the
outcome of the race was uncertain and the popular vote quite close. In
both 1960 and 1968, the Democratic Party offered candidates who
were associated with progressive stands on civil rights and racial issues,[31] and this might be responsible for the decrease in efficacy differences between black and white women. Differences in turnout between black and white women also diminish, especially by 1968.

There are also participation differences between black and white
women with high school educations (see Table 28). White women,
participate more than black women, in most cases, in voting and electoral participation, in conventional activism, and in political involvement. In voting participation, white-black differences diminish over
time but do not disappear, as they do for grade school educated women.
In electoral participation, differences are generally slightly greater than
5 percent, except for 1968 and 1972, when differences disappear. Differences in conventional activism are much greater, especially by 1976.[32]
For involvement, differences vary, depending upon the year but, except for 1964 and 1972 (when the outcomes of the elections were
predictable and overwhelming), involvement differences are approxi-
mately 10 percent.

As is the case with poorly educated black women, high school educated black women are more supportive of unconventional activism
than are their white counterparts; however, the differences are greater
in this case than they are for the grade school educated. With political
efficacy, race related differences are small, vary across time, and vary
in direction.[33]

In making these comparisons between black and white women, it is
important to note that, for white women, education makes more of a
difference in political participation than it does for black women—at
least when the levels of educational attainment being compared are

Table 27.
Percent Active, and Total Number of, Respondents, by Gender and Race: Grade School Educated

	1952 Women	1952 Men	1956 Women	1956 Men	1960 Women	1960 Men	1964 Women	1964 Men	1968 Women	1968 Men	1972 Women	1972 Men	1976 Women	1976 Men
VOTING[a]														
whites	*	*	58.2% (244)	75.3% (219)	58.6% (70)	78.8% (66)	69.5% (141)	73.3% (150)	58.2% (134)	61.5% (122)	50.2% (201)	70.2% (171)	50.2% (148)	71.9% (144)
blacks	*	*	16.7 (42)	35.3 (34)	34.8 (23)	40.9 (22)	50.0 (36)	60.9 (23)	57.1 (28)	82.6 (23)	52.8 (36)	53.8 (26)	51.4 (525)	85.7 (175)
ELECTORAL PARTICIPATION														
whites	5.5 (272)	8.9 (271)	6.6 (242)	11.0 (219)	6.3 (64)	13.3 (60)	2.2 (139)	8.1 (149)	9.0 (122)	13.7 (117)	3.6 (193)	11.0 (164)	5.6 (144)	7.2 (138)
blacks	1.8 (56)	8.9 (51)	4.8 (42)	2.9 (34)	10.0 (20)	4.8 (21)	0.0 (34)	13.0 (23)	3.6 (28)	4.3 (23)	0.0 (36)	7.7 (26)	5.7 (53)	**
CONVENTIONAL ACTIVISM														
whites	*	*	*	*	*	*	7.1 (141)	10.1 (149)	5.5 (127)	14.0 (121)	10.4 (193)	15.3 (163)	9.4 (144)	18.2 (143)
blacks	*	*	*	*	*	*	0.0 (35)	0.0 (23)	0.0 (28)	4.3 (23)	2.8 (36)	11.5 (26)	0.0 (53)	**

*No data are available of these variables for these years.

**N<20.

[a]Voting levels for 1952 are exaggerated, and hence are not included here.

	1952		1956		1960		1964		1968		1972		1976	
	Women	Men	Women	Men	Women	Men	Women	Men	Women	Men	Women	Men	Women	Men
UNCONVENTIONAL ACTIVISM[b]														
whites	*	*	*	*	*	*	*	*	11.5% (87)	4.4% (90)	5.5% (217)	4.7% (191)	0.0% (189)	0.0% (187)
blacks	*	*	*	*	*	*	*	*	45.5 (22)	**	25.0 (32)	17.9 (28)	0.0 (60)	0.0 (22)
POLITICAL INVOLVEMENT														
whites	6.7 (268)	12.8 (265)	4.1 (241)	9.6 (218)	22.9 (61)	28.3 (60)	10.8 (139)	11.4 (149)	6.4 (125)	8.4 (119)	17.5 (101)	18.4 (87)	19.6 (143)	28.1 (143)
blacks	0.0 (53)	6.3 (48)	0.0 (41)	6.3 (32)	20.0 (20)	19.0 (21)	0.0 (36)	8.7 (23)	3.8 (26)	4.3 (23)	16.7 (12)	**	18.4 (52)	**
POLITICAL EFFICACY[c]														
whites	13.7 (299)	22.8 (303)	10.9 (238)	30.2 (212)	10.1 (69)	32.8 (64)	10.7 (149)	16.0 (163)	30.3 (145)	35.3 (139)	7.4 (244)	14.7 (204)	5.9 (144)	14.9 (138)
blacks	5.5 (55)	17.3 (52)	5.1 (39)	5.9 (34)	21.7 (23)	14.3 (21)	8.1 (37)	13.0 (23)	44.1 (34)	68.0 (25)	10.3 (39)	13.3 (30)	23.2 (48)	**

*No data are available for these variables for these years.

**N<20.

[b]Note that unconventional activism is measured as support for such participation in 1968 and 1972, and as actual unconventional participation in 1976.

[c]A change in question-wording for 1968 exaggerates the proportion of efficacious respondents.

137

Table 28.
Percent Active, and Total Number of, Respondents, by Gender and Race: High School Educated

	1952 Women	1952 Men	1956 Women	1956 Men	1960 Women	1960 Men	1964 Women	1964 Men	1968 Women	1968 Men	1972 Women	1972 Men	1976 Women	1976 Men
VOTING[a]														
whites	*	*	73.0% (488)	82.3% (333)	76.7% (390)	83.2% (316)	77.0% (409)	83.3% (269)	79.8% (376)	79.7% (231)	69.1% (643)	73.9% (376)	66.3% (686)	68.6% (374)
blacks	*	*	35.9 (39)	**	33.3 (24)	**	68.8 (48)	**	62.2 (45)	**	59.3 (81)	71.4 (35)	52.3 (66)	76.7 (30)
ELECTORAL ACTIVISM														
whites	9.0 (312)	12.1 (223)	12.7 (487)	16.8 (333)	15.0 (359)	16.8 (298)	14.8 (406)	13.5 (266)	14.4 (355)	12.0 (217)	12.7 (612)	14.2 (365)	10.9 (632)	10.6 (345)
blacks	4.5 (22)	**	5.1 (39)	**	13.6 (22)	**	6.4 (47)	**	14.6 (41)	**	15.6 (77)	11.8 (34)	3.0 (66)	30.9 (28)
CONVENTIONAL ACTIVISM														
whites	*	*	*	*	*	*	16.7 (408)	16.0 (269)	16.0 (362)	18.5 (222)	25.5 (612)	26.2 (367)	25.1 (680)	27.7 (371)
blacks	*	*	*	*	*	*	4.2 (48)	**	4.5 (44)	**	13.0 (77)	8.8 (34)	1.6 (64)	20.0 (30)

*No data are available for these variables for these years.

**N<20.

[a]Voting levels are exaggerated in 1952, and hence are not included here.

	1952		1956		1960		1964		1968		1972		1976	
	Women	Men	Women	Men	Women	Men	Women	Men	Women	Men	Women	Men	Women	Men
UNCONVENTIONAL ACTIVISM[b]														
whites	*	*	*	*	*	*	*	*	10.5% (313)	5.5% (201)	10.2% (733)	10.7% (448)	0.4% (779)	0.2% (46)
blacks	*	*	*	*	*	*	*	*	25.0 (28)	**	18.5 (92)	39.0 (41)	0.0 (95)	0.0 (45)
POLITICAL INVOLVEMENT														
whites	24.4 (307)	30.1 (307)	13.2 (485)	17.0 (329)	36.0 (344)	42.5 (285)	18.2 (406)	22.8 (267)	18.3 (355)	19.1 (220)	19.3 (301)	22.5 (187)	26.5 (679)	31.4 (368)
blacks	9.1 (22)	**	5.3 (38)	**	19.0 (21)	**	16.7 (48)	**	7.0 (43)	**	19.0 (42)	**	16.7 (66)	48.3 (30)
POLITICAL EFFICACY[c]														
whites	19.2 (343)	41.6 (243)	33.9 (484)	41.8 (330)	36.2 (376)	47.6 (307)	24.6 (426)	38.5 (283)	50.4 (421)	60.4 (255)	18.5 (756)	28.5 (456)	17.2 (675)	27.3 (370)
blacks	20.0 (25)	**	25.6 (39)	**	23.8 (21)	**	26.0 (50)	31.8 (22)	55.6 (45)	65.0 (20)	10.3 (97)	30.2 (43)	24.6 (63)	15.0 (30)

*No data are available for these variables for these years.

**N<20.

[b]Note that unconventional participation is measured as support for such activism in 1968 and 1972, and as actual participation in 1976.

[c]Efficacy levels are exaggerated in 1968, due to a change in question-wording.

below the college level. However, black women with high school educations participate just as much—or just about as little—as their sisters with grade school educations. After 1968, voting levels for black women of different educational attainment are similar; there are similar levels of participation in electoral activities, political involvement (depending upon the year), and, by 1972, of political efficacy. The only dramatic difference between grade school educated and high school educated black women is for approval of unconventional activism. Both groups of black women are more supportive of this kind of activity than their white counterparts, but black women with high school educations are much more supportive, especially in 1968.[34]

Again, the problem of small numbers of blacks in any sample year restricts the kinds of controls that we can place on relationships. It may be that while high school educations do not contribute as much to black women's participation as they do to white women's, attainment of some college education makes an overwhelming—or overwhelmingly similar—difference for black women. The fact that high school educations do not seem to contribute to black women's political participation may, however, be a reflection of the race related differences in educational quality in the United States. While black and white women may have similar levels of educational attainment, white women may receive a better quality of education than do black women. It may not be the level of educational attainment as much as the type of education to which women of different races have access. Inequality of education—even when there is "equality" in level of educational attainment—may make such comparisons inadequate.

Race Related Participation Differences between Women and Men

We suggested earlier an hypothesis that gender related differences in participation among blacks should be smaller than gender related differences in participation among whites—due, primarily, to the differences in gender-role socialization for white girls and for black girls. We will attempt to assess that hypothesis despite the fact that a comparison of race related participation differences for women and men is made difficult (and, in some cases, impossible) by the small numbers of blacks in each sample, especially by the small numbers of black men.

Among those with grade school educations, it is not clear that there are fewer gender related participation differences among blacks than there are for whites. An examination of the average percentage participation differences across years, for those years where there are at least twenty-five black male respondents, shows that the patterns for blacks and for whites are similar for all types of participation, involvement, and efficacy (see again Table 27). In almost all cases, men report being more active, involved, and efficacious than do women, although the pattern for gender related differences for blacks is not always consistent and is, again, confounded by the small numbers problem. The only exception to the evidence of men's greater activism is in support for unconventional activities: women of both races are slightly more supportive of such participation than are men.

Among those who have at least some high school education, the patterns are less clear, but the average percentage participation differences suggest a somewhat dissimilar picture (see again Table 28). Among whites, men and women appear equally participant in electoral and conventional activism, with similar levels of support for unconventional activities (although women are very slightly more supportive) and of political involvement. Only for political efficacy is there an average percentage difference greater than 5 percent. Among blacks, the pattern is less clear because of the problem of small numbers of black males in the samples. It appears that black men are more active than their female counterparts in voting, electoral participation, support for unconventional behavior, political involvement, and political efficacy. However, both black women and black men are unlikely to participate in conventional activities. Note that the average number of black male respondents with high school educations is twenty-four, making comparisons unreliable.

It is highly likely that the black men (and women) in the samples are unrepresentative of black people in America;[35] the suggestion that black men are more active politically than black women is contradicted by other studies.[36] Members of the black community have attempted to resolve the small numbers problem that is inherent in mass survey polling by establishing their own polling organizations, since most nationwide samples "will include no more than 150 to 200 blacks. With such a small number, it is difficult simply to be certain about the accuracy of findings from the total black sample; it is virtually impossible to break down the sample into subgroups, to know more about the complexity of black opinion."[37]

In addition, "the inability to break black opinion into its economic and social components . . . feeds the idea that blacks are an undifferentiated mass and should be treated as such."[38]

More issues remain unsettled, using the ICPSR data, than have been resolved. Black women in the United States are socialized differently than white women. However, the suggestion that this difference in socialization should result in participation similarities cannot be accepted; given the limitations of the data, there is not sufficient evidence here to conclude that such an assertion can be rejected. Second, the claim that there should be fewer gender related differences in participation among blacks than among whites likewise cannot be accepted. These data suggest that there are at least as many—and as great—gender related differences among blacks as there are among whites. Here, however, the data are even weaker, given that there are so few black men in the samples. Again, this issue remains unresolved by these data.

NOTES

1. Herbert H. Hyman writes: "At early ages, boys are directed toward politics, and here lie the seeds of adult differentiations everywhere found in studies of political participation." See Herbert H. Hyman, *Political Socialization* (Glencoe,Ill.: The Free Press, 1959), p. 31.

2. While none of the authors who use the term "patriarchal" offers a definition, it has been generally used to mean the rule of women by men. Among feminist theorists, Sheila Rowbotham states, "Patriarchal control is based on male control over the woman's productive capacity, and over her person." Sheila Rowbotham, *Woman's Consciousness, Man's World* (Middlesex, Eng.: Penguin, 1973), p. 117. Zillah Eisenstein writes: "Patriarchy as a political structure seeks to control and subjugate women so that their possibilities for making choices about their sexuality, childrearing, mothering, loving and laboring are curtailed," and elsewhere equates patriarchy with "the hierarchical sex organization of . . . society." See Zillah Eisenstein, *The Radical Future of Liberal Feminism* (New York: Longman, 1981), pp. 14 and 22.

3. S. M. Miller and Frank Riessman, "The Working Class Subculture: A New View," in Paul Blumberg, ed., *The Impact of Social Class* (New York: Thomas Y. Crowell, 1972), p. 191.

4. Donald McKinley, *Social Class and Family Life* (London: The Free Press, 1964), p. 89.

5. Ibid.

6. Helen Mayer Hacker,"Class and Race Differences in Gender Roles," in Lucile Duberman, *Gender and Sex in Society* (New York: Praeger, 1975), p. 147.

7. Lee Rainwater, Richard P. Coleman, and Gerald Handel, "The Workingman's Wife: Day In, Day Out," in Blumberg, *The Impact of Social Class*, p. 440.

8. Paul Blumberg, in his brief introduction to the Rainwater et al. essay in *The Impact of Social Class*, p. 440 might be accused himself of "sparse intellectual resources," for his blithe blanket description of working-class women's intelligence. The Rainwater study was completed in 1959; since that time, the lives of working-class wives have changed with their entrance in increasing numbers into the work force. To argue now that the working-class wife leads an existence sheltered and isolated from most of the world is to ignore the fact that most working-class *wives* are now working-class *workers*.

9. Hacker, "Class and Race," p. 146. See also Irene Frieze and various authors, *Women and Sex Roles: A Social Psychological Perspective* (New York: W. W. Norton, 1978), p. 288.

10. This question, for the years 1956–1968 and 1976, is coded as "middle class" (excluding responses of "upper class," of which there were nine, for example, in 1976), and "working class" (including responses of "lower or 'poor' class," of which there were sixteen in 1976). Twelve respondents who gave some "other" class background were recoded as missing data.

11. There are no differences in support for, or participation in, unconventional activism between these two groups.

12. An alternative explanation, which cannot be verified, is that adult socialization—experience in the work force or the resocializing influence of a college education—has overridden whatever class socialization the respondent may have received in childhood. For a discussion of childhood and adult socialization of women, see Virginia Sapiro, *The Political Integration of Women* (Champaign, Ill.: University of Illinois Press, 1983), Chapter 3.

13. Note that, in certain cases, middle-class women are slightly *more* politically involved than their male counterparts, although these differences are not large.

14. Note that working-class women are slightly more supportive of unconventional activism than are men in 1968.

15. A potential relationship between women's class background and political participation may be obscured by women's subjective class status, at least for those women who are married. The issue of class identification for women is difficult, since most women do not have a class status of their own, but one derived primarily from their father and, when they marry, from their husband. For a discussion of derived social status, see Eileen McDonagh, "To Work or Not To Work: The Differential Impact of Achieved and Derived Status upon the Political Participation of Women, 1956–1976," *American Journal of Political Science*, XXVI (2), May 1982, pp. 280–297.

If class background is a useful surrogate of women's socialization and if childhood socialization is not superseded by adult socialization experiences, we should find lower levels of participation among women of working-class backgrounds who are married to middle-class men than we find among their middle-class counterparts who married within their class. We should also expect to find higher levels of participation among women from middle-class backgrounds who married working-class men than we would find among their working-class counterparts with working-class husbands. The problem of small numbers confounds an examination of these questions; for most survey years, however, the majority of respondents—male and female—marry within the class in which they grew up.

Artemis March notes the difficulty in assigning "class status" to women:

The subsumption of women into classes distorts social organization generally, and stratification specifically. An adequate account of women and class has yet to be developed, and requires a much greater understanding of gender relations than we have now. In other words, the question of women and class is in many ways premature, and the ellision of women into male classes has the effect of perpetuating female invisibility."

See Artemis March, "Female Invisibility in Androcentric Sociological Theory," paper presented at the 1978 meetings of the American Sociological Association, quoted in Jessie Bernard, *The Female World* (New York: The Free Press, 1981), p. 232.

16.   See Angela Davis, "Reflections on the Black Woman's Role in the Community of Slaves," *The Black Scholar*, III (4), December 1971, pp. 2–15.

17.   Virginia O'Leary, *Toward Understanding Women* (Monterey, Calif.: Brooks/Cole, 1977), p. 136.

18.   Ibid. See also Frieze et al., *Women and Sex Roles*, p. 288–289.

19.   O'Leary, *Toward Understanding Women*, p. 138.

20.   Ibid., p. 140.

21.   Ibid., p. 145. See also Carrie Allen McCray, "The Black Woman and Family Roles," in LaFrances Rodgers-Rose, ed., *The Black Woman* (Beverly Hills: Sage, 1980), pp. 67–78.

22.   For a similar argument, see Michelle Wallace, *Black Macho and the Myth of the Superwoman* (New York: Dial, 1978).

23.   See also Erlene Stetson, "Silence: Access and Aspiration," in Carol Ascher, Louise DeSalvo, and Sara Ruddick, eds., *Between Women* (Boston: Beacon Press, 1984), pp. 237–251, especially pp. 237–238, on the need to understand black women as a group different from black *men* and *white* women.

24.   See Richard Cloward and Frances Fox Piven, "Hidden Protest: The Channeling of Female Innovation and Resistance," in *Signs*, IV (4), 1979, pp. 651–669, for general mention of hardship conditions of women which should provide stress and hence deviant behavior (as much of the literature suggests) but in fact do not result in such behavior; they attempt to answer the question of "why women deviate as little as they do." In the case of black

women, hardship conditions should depress political participation, but in many instances black women participate more than would be expected; we need to ask, then, the question of "why black women participate as much as they do."

25. See John C. Pierce, William P. Avery, and Addison Carey, Jr., "Sex Differences in Black Political Beliefs and Behavior," *American Journal of Political Science*, XVII (2), May 1973, pp. 422–430.

26. See again Stetson, "Silence: Access and Aspiration;" and Daniel P. Moynihan, *The Negro Family: The Case for National Action* (Washington, D.C.: U.S. Department of Labor, 1965), as an example of the kind of writing on black women which Stetson condemns.

27. For a discussion of the small numbers of black respondents problem, see E. J. Dionne, "Pollsters Do Their Numbers on What Black America Thinks," *New York Times*, January 20, 1980.

28. For a description of parochial participation, see Sidney Verba and Norman H. Nie, *Participation in America: Political Democracy and Social Equality* (New York: Harper and Row, 1972), Chapter 4. For black representation among parochial participants, see especially pp. 99 and 151.

29. See Lester Milbrath and M. L. Goel, *Political Participation*, 3d ed. (New York: Rand McNally, 1977), pp. 14–15 and 70–71.

30. Keep in mind the low numbers of black women in this category. Also, note that there is a problem with the efficacy question for 1968. In that year, the question was: "Would you say that politics and government are so complicated that people like you can't really understand what's going on, or that you can understand what's going on pretty well?" Of those responding, 55.5 percent (844) said that they understood contemporary politics; 45.5 percent (677) responded that they did not. In all other years of study, the question asked for agreement or disagreement with the statement: "Sometimes politics and government seem so complicated that a person like me can't really understand what's going on." In 1976, for example, 72.7 percent (1,710) agreed with the statement, while only 27.3 percent disagreed. It is more likely that the form of the question evoked more positive answers in 1968 than the original question when asked in other years; it is less likely that such an unusually large percentage of Americans felt particularly efficacious in 1968.

31. Both John F. Kennedy (1960) and Hubert H. Humphrey (1968) made campaign appeals to black voters; in each case, the opposing Republican candidate for president was Richard M. Nixon, and in each case, the results of the popular vote were very close. In 1960, Kennedy received 49.9 percent of the popular vote to Nixon's 49.6 percent; in 1968, Humphrey received 42.7 percent of the popular vote to Nixon's 43.4 percent. For a discussion of the strategy of the Kennedy campaign in regard to black voters, see Frances Fox Piven and Richard Cloward, *Poor People's Movement* (New York: Vintage, 1979), Chapter 4.

32. See again Verba and Nie, *Participation in America*, pp. 98 and 151.

33. Note again the problem with the political efficacy measure for 1968; see fn. 30.

34. Piven and Cloward, in *Poor People's Movements*, Introduction and Chapter 1, argue that unconventional activism has been particularly effective for the poor and for blacks.

35. See Dionne, "Pollsters."

36. See Pierce et al., "Sex Differences in Black Political Beliefs and Behavior."

37. Dionne, "Pollsters."

38. Ibid.

CHAPTER VII

WOMEN'S POLITICAL PARTICIPATION: CONCLUSIONS AND POSSIBILITIES

The most striking characteristic of American political participation, for men or for women, is just how little political participation there is to be explained in the United States. Voting levels are, of course, exaggerated in mass surveys, presumably as respondents give the "correct" civic duty reply to questions about voting behavior. Americans, despite our "civic culture,"[1] have relatively low levels of voting participation in comparison to other Western industrialized nations.[2] There is a variety of potential explanations for this decline in voting participation in the United States: the lack of choice offered by two major political parties which dominate not only the party system but the electoral system;[3] the decline of confidence and trust of the American people in political and other elites;[4] the decrease in Americans' feelings of political efficacy;[5] and certain structural barriers, such as restrictive registration requirements or the inconvenience of traveling to the polls on a working day.[6] Whatever the source or sources for the decline in voting participation, this decline ought to concern us for two reasons. First, voting is presumably the "simplest" political act in which masses of American citizens engage; and if there is a constant decline in voting participation, we can hardly expect good news about other, perhaps more difficult, forms of political participation. Second, democracy depends upon citizen participation; even the claims of "democratic revisionists" or democratic elitists require that, at the very least, democracy be approximated by the periodic participation of the citizenry in its choice of political elites.[7] Constant decline of voting participation may be interpreted as a serious challenge to the claims of democratic elitists that Americans "approximate democracy." It may be also interpreted as a challenge to the legitimacy of government.[8] Low levels of political involvement and feelings of political efficacy may be interpreted in the same way.

Any conclusions about the mass-level political participation of American women need to be drawn in the context of this larger discussion concerning the relatively low, and declining, levels of mass political activism in the United States. The conclusions which we have drawn thus far should concern us. First, as we demonstrated in Chapter II, there are few mass-level differences in political participation between women and men; what differences exist are modest and weak. In this regard, women's participation mirrors the unimpressive (and sometimes impressively low) level of men's activism.[9] This is the case when we examine the bivariate relationship between participation and gender; the case is maintained when we examine subgroups by gender.

Table 29 provides a gross summary of the average percentage of active respondents, by gender, across all years for which data are available.[10] These data confirm the general *similarity* of mass-level participation, by gender. What few differences exist demonstrate no particular pattern, and for only ten of the sixty-five instances displayed are percentage differences greater than 9 percent—with one major exception.

There is one area of political behavior where women are disproportionately present: women are strongly, consistently present among those who report agreement with the statement that "politics and government are too complicated for a person like me to understand"—a presence which does not vary by subgroup. For all subgroups presented in Table 29, at least 10 percent fewer women report feelings of political efficacy than men, and in most subgroups the percentage difference is much higher. It is for feelings of political efficacy that gender related differences appear to be greatest; regardless of a variety of controls, as a group, women report lower levels of efficacy than do men.

Table 30 shows the percentage of women who reported disagreement with the efficacy statement in the 1976 survey (the percentage of women who reported feeling efficacious). In 1976, the reported efficacy levels of all groups of women were remarkably similar, except for women with many children and blue-collar working women, and all were remarkably low. Only professionally employed women and

Table 29.
Average Percent Active Respondents, Male and Female, for Years for Which Data Are Available

	Vote[b]	Electoral Activism[b]	Conventional Activism[c]	Involvement[b]	Efficacy[b]
OCCUPATION:					
Professionals	83.3%	24.0%	37.8%	35.0%	41.8%
	(88.7)	(25.5)	(40.1)	(40.0)	(59.8)
Clericals	80.8	17.3	25.1	25.6	38.2
	(89.1)	(19.9)	(35.8)	(35.4)	(53.7)
Blue-collar	62.6	8.6	12.7	12.6	19.3
Workers	(72.0)	(12.1)	(18.1)	(20.6)	(35.8)
Housewives	69.8	13.2	20.6	22.9	28.3
NUMBER OF CHILDREN[d]					
None	72.5	14.4	21.2	23.2	30.2
	(77.2)	(15.8)	(23.9)	(26.7)	(44.9)
One	69.6	16.8	19.7	22.9	28.9
	(80.1)	(13.9)	(20.7)	(23.8)	(42.4)
Two	74.9	13.7	21.2	20.4	30.3
	(80.0)	(22.2)	(31.1)	(29.9)	(51.0)
Three	71.1	13.6	25.0	23.1	30.1
	(82.6)	(18.3)	(32.2)	(27.3)	(44.9)
Four or More	62.7	14.7	16.0	18.1	21.0
	(79.4)	(17.1)	(21.8)	(24.6)	(42.7)
SOCIAL CLASS BACKGROUND[d]					
Middle-Class	80.6	22.5	28.9	32.8	45.9
	(85.0)	(22.8)	(30.0)	(38.4)	(55.5)
Working-Class	67.6	11.0	16.6	17.1	28.6
	(77.2)	(14.6)	(23.5)	(22.7)	(40.2)
RACE[b]					
White	73.8	14.7	24.2	23.0	20.8
	(80.2)	(19.9)	(28.3)	(28.0)	(43.5)
Black	52.7	9.0	7.6	12.9	21.3
	(64.7)	(13.8)	(10.5)	(22.0)	(31.2)

[a] Men's responses are in parentheses.　　[b] Data available for 1952-1976.
[c] Data available for 1964-1976.　　[d] Data available for 1956-1968, 1976.

Table 30.

Percentage of Women Reporting Disagreement with the Assertion that Politics and Government Are Too Complicated to Understand, for Various Groups, 1976

	Percent Efficacious (In Disagreement)
Women from middle-class family backgrounds	27.2%
Women from working-class family backgrounds	18.5%
Black women	25.1%
White women	21.3%
Professional women	33.3%
Clerical women	23.2%
Skilled working women	9.8%
Unskilled working women	6.4%
Housewives	19.7%
Women with no children	25.7%
Women with one child	22.2%
Women with two children	23.4%
Women with three children	22.1%
Women with four children	12.5%
Feminists[a]	30.5%

[a]Those who ranked "most feminist" in support of feminist issues.

feminists show relatively high levels of political efficacy—and even here there is considerably less than a majority feeling confident about their political abilities.

If we are concerned about low levels of mass political activism in the United States, and if our concern is specifically with increasing women's political participation, this study provides us with some modest instruction. First, there are no unique sources of women's political participation—at least in terms of the forms of participation investigated here—which we could utilize to help mobilize women for political change.[11] Our data do not allow us to claim with any certainty that the presence of a visible and active feminist movement will help mobilize women beyond its general mobilizing impact upon men (see Chapter IV). Employment outside the home in a white-collar position (see Chapter III) and identifying with the contemporary feminist movement and supporting feminist issues (see Chapter V) are positively related to mass-level political participation but, again, no more so for women than for men. There are some few intersections of life conditions, however, which may have positive and specific impacts upon women's mass-level participation: for example, women who are college educated and supportive of feminist issues report higher levels for some kinds of political activism than their male peers and than other women (see Chapter V).

On the other hand, there are certain life circumstances which are specifically debilitating to women's political participation: large numbers of children at home and employment outside the home as a blue-collar worker are both relatively, dramatically disabling to women's participation in mass politics (see Chapter III). Two of the strongest predictors of low levels of political participation for women are social class background and race; that is, black women and women from the working class are the least active women, particularly among the poorly educated, in each sample year. The consistency and magnitude of their inactivism is striking across the twenty-four-year period examined here. Only in 1976 are the differences between these women and other women modest, and only in the case of political efficacy.

The differences in mass-level political participation are greater among women than they are between women and men. Groups of women vary considerably in their level of political activism.[12] Professionally employed women and female clericals, middle-class women, and white women consistently report higher voting levels than do other groups of women, especially black women, working-class women, and women with four or more children.

A somewhat similar pattern is found for electoral activism. The groups with the highest percentages of electoral activists are professional women (37.0 percent in 1960 and 35.9 percent in 1964), clerical workers (28.2 percent in 1960), and women from middle-class family backgrounds (27.7 percent in 1960). Considering that electoral activism is measured by an index of three indicators and that, for percentage comparisons, electoral activists include everyone who scored positively on at least one of these indicators, even the largest percentages of women active are hardly testimony to massive electoral activism among women in the United States, and the limited number of groups of female activists is not reassuring. Those groups of women who participate least in electoral activities are skilled and unskilled female workers (the average electoral participation rate across all years is 8.7 and 8.6 percent, respectively), women from a working-class family background (11.0 average percent active), and black women (9.0 average percent active). Given that these who tend to be the least advantaged economically and educationally in society—blacks, those from the working class, and blue-collar workers—do not participate in electoral politics in large numbers, we can take little solace from the assurances of democratic elitists that the needs of these women will be "anticipated" and hence met.[13]

The pattern for women's conventional activism may be interpreted similarly. Professionally employed women, whites, and middle-class women were among the most active, while conventional participation was lowest among blue-collar working women and black women. Conventional participation among black women was lower than that of any other group of women (the average percent active across the four data years is 7.6).[14]

Protest and demonstration activity and civil disobedience are well-called "unconventional" forms of participation, since, indeed, few Americans engage in such activities. Verba and Nie do not include a discussion of this type of activism in their *Participation in America*.[15] Very few women, regardless of life situation, approve of or engage in unconventional activism.[16] There is, again, considerably more support for such activities than there is participation in them. The most support for unconventional activism came from grade school educated black women: 45.5 percent in 1968 and 25.0 percent in 1972. Also supportive of unconventional activism were professionally employed women (24.4 percent in 1968), college educated, middle-class women (26.0 percent in 1968), and high school educated black women (25.0 percent in 1968). For none of these groups is their approval of unconventional activism matched by a concomitant participation, including grade school educated black women.

One of the most important changes in American political attitudes since the 1960s has been the decline of public trust in political and other elites.[17] This decline, concurrent with the decrease in mass political participation, raises serious questions about the extent to which Americans grant legitimacy to the government. Among women, those groups of women most active in voting and in electoral and conventional nonelectoral participation, are those most "involved" in politics; that is, they are disproportionately present among those who follow politics through the media and who express political interest.[18] White-collar workers, women from middle-class family backgrounds, and women with one or fewer children are most involved (in 1960, 54.3 percent for professionally employed women, 38.8 percent for clerical workers, 50.0 percent for middle-class women, regardless of level of education, and 40.7 percent, and 39.1 percent, for women with one or no child, respectively). Those women who are least active also are underrepresented among the politically involved: blue-collar workers and blacks. While the pattern of difference among subgroups of women varies considerably across years, the general pattern is confirmed for political involvement as well.

We have already discussed the case for political efficacy (see Table 30). By 1976, the differences in political efficacy among subgroups of women are modest. However, the general pattern again holds: those who participate most among women are the most efficacious (although, again, we are not talking about high levels of political efficacy among women of any subgroup, for any year). Professional and clerical working women and women from middle-class backgrounds report higher proportions of efficacy responses than do other groups (50.0 percent, 56.0 percent, and 47.9 percent in 1960, respectively), while blue-collar working women and women with many children have the lowest proportion of efficacious responses, especially by 1976.

The low levels of women reporting feelings of political efficacy are especially interesting. First, it is for feelings of political efficacy that gender related differences appear to be greatest; regardless of a variety of controls, women report lower levels of efficacy than do men, even where subgroups of men report low levels of efficacy. Second, by 1976, the reported efficacy levels of all groups of women were remarkably similar (with the exceptions of women with many children and blue-collar working women; see again Table 30). Controls for education do not eliminate the relationship between efficacy and gender. While some groups of women report higher levels of efficacy than others, the differences are not great—and gender related differences persist, despite a variety of controls.[19] What is additionally unique is that while the similarities among groups of women and the differences between women and men are greatest for this variable, they are not reflected in such great strength for other political predispositions or behaviors. Gender related differences in political efficacy persist, even when actual participation differences are negligible.

CHANGING SOURCES OF WOMEN'S POLITICAL PARTICIPATION?

There are two possible changes in the sources of women's political participation: first, that some sources have been more or less important at different times and, second, that some sources are more important to certain kinds of participation than others. We may assess these possibilities by examining the relationship between the independent variables claimed to be unique to women's participation and activism, over the twenty-four-year time span, controlled for a variety of demographic variables. The data are presented in Table 31; they reveal the following. First, none of the independent variables under investigation serves fully to explain women's participation. The relationship between each independent variable and each type of participation for every year is relatively weak and, indeed, in most cases, the relationship between each variable and each type of participation is stronger for men than it is for women. The variables taken jointly, for each type of participation for 1952 to 1976, explain little.

There has been some change over time, however. The variables, taken jointly, become increasingly strongly related to voting participation across time, with varying levels of significance; this is true for men as it is for women. However, occupational status accounts for most of the change; number of children, generation, and support for feminist issues explain little. Feminism, as noted in Chapter V, is unrelated to voting for both women and men.

The pattern is similar for electoral activism. The variables taken jointly explain very little, although by 1964 the relationship becomes stronger and statistically significant. Occupational status again explains most of the relationship, at least until 1972; then women's support for feminist issues becomes equally important and statistically significant. Number of children and generation are not strongly related to electoral activism among women or men.

A conventional activism measure is not available until 1964. The independent variables taken jointly explain very little about women's political participation; in fact, they explain more for men. A clear pattern does not emerge over the four data years, but, again, occupation explains most of the relationship. Neither number of children nor generation is particularly useful in explaining women's conventional nonelectoral participation.

Again, unconventional activism is measured by approval of such participation in 1968 and 1972 and by actual participation in 1976. All variables taken jointly explain most of the support for unconventional activities in 1968, while support for feminist issues is most strongly related to women's support for unconventional activism in 1972. In 1976, women's work variables—occupational status and number of children—explain most about women's actual protest participation, while they are unrelated to men's unconventional activism.

In regard to women's political involvement, the variables taken jointly explain the most, with occupational status making the greatest contribution (although this is more true for men than for women). Support for feminist issues contributes equally to explaining women's political involvement in 1972. Likewise, feelings of political efficacy among women can be explained by the joint contribution of the independent variables, with the relationship varying in strength throughout the 1960s and 1970s; the pattern for political efficacy among women is similar to that for women's political involvement. Again, occupational status and support for feminist issues contribute the most individually to an explanation of women's political efficacy, while generation and number of children are apparently unrelated. All of the independent variables, however, are more useful for explaining men's feelings about involvement and efficacy.

There are several points to be noted about the usefulness of these variables. The first is that women's work explains surprisingly little about women's political participation, broadly conceived; and certainly it explains less for women than for men, even when one includes considerations of housewifery and childcare. This may be in part the result of the problems of evaluating housewifery as an occupational variable, since married women who are employed for pay outside the home remain housewives, and since some housewives have resources for political participation derived from their husbands. Other problems of using these particular mass survey data to measure occupation may be related to the changes in women's work over the past decades, characterized not only by the increase in numbers of women employed outside the home but by the increasing "ghetto-ization" of

Table 31.
The Uncontrolled Relationships between Participation and Women's Work, Political Generation, and Feminism, by Gender

	1952 Women	1952 Men	1956 Women	1956 Men	1960 Women	1960 Men	1964 Women	1964 Men	1968 Women	1968 Men	1972 Women	1972 Men	1976 Women	1976 Men
VOTING														
Occupation	.05	.10[a]	.10[b]	.17[c]	.13[c]	.17[b]	.08	.17[c]	.08	.15[b]	.18[c]	.12[a]	.08	.22[c]
Number of children	*	*	.12[c]	.05	.11[a]	.04	.05	.01	.05	.12[a]	*	*	-.13[b]	-.16[c]
Generation	.01	-.00	-.10[b]	-.05	-.02	-.07	.09[a]	.13[b]	.26[c]	.13[a]	.10[a]	.14[a]	.21[c]	.26[c]
Feminism	*	*	*	*	*	*	*	*	*	*	.07	-.03	.02	-.06
All models	.06	.11[a]	.17[a]	.21[a]	.17[a]	.20[b]	.14[a]	.26[c]	.27[c]	.27[c]	.29[c]	.26[a]	.28[b]	.36[c]
ELECTORAL PARTICIPATION														
Occupation	.02	.26[c]	.10[a]	.10[a]	.19[c]	.05	.17[c]	.23[c]	.05	.17[b]	.15[c]	.14[b]	.09[a]	.14[b]
Number of children	*	*	-.02	.01	.02	-.02	-.06	.04	-.01	-.00	*	*	.01	-.02
Generation	-.02	.05	-.01	-.05	.02	-.04	.03	.01	.03	.09	.00	.07	.09[a]	.16[c]
Feminism	*	*	*	*	*	*	*	*	*	*	.16[c]	.03	.10[a]	.11[a]
All models	.07	.28[c]	.08	.11	.17[a]	.11	.23[c]	.29[c]	.20[a]	.26[c]	.18[c]	.20[a]	.18	.21[a]
CONVENTIONAL ACTIVISM														
Occupation	*	*	*	*	*	*	.06	.23[c]	-.03	.14[b]	.22[c]	.18[b]	.17[c]	.19[c]
Number of children	*	*	*	*	*	*	.08[a]	-.04	.03	-.05	*	*	-.06	-.08
Generation	*	*	*	*	*	*	.06	.02	.06	.03	.01	.10	.11[a]	.12[b]
Feminism	*	*	*	*	*	*	*	*	*	*	.37[c]	.15[b]	.06[a]	.06
All models	*	*	*	*	*	*	.14[a]	.23[c]	.18[a]	.19[a]	.19[a]	.19[a]	.17	.24[a]

*No data available for these variables for these years.

Note: Figures presented are standardized regression coefficients for occupation, number of children, generation, and feminism; multiple Rs are presented for "all models," or the joint influence of all independent variables upon participation. Data concerning number of children are not available for 1952 and 1972; data concerning "feminism"(support for feminist issues) are available in 1972 and 1976 only.

[a] p < .05.   [b] p < .01.   [c] p < .001.

	1952		1956		1960		1964		1968		1972		1976	
	Women	Men	Women	Men	Women	Men	Women	Men	Women	Men	Women	Men	Women	Men
UNCONVENTIONAL ACTIVISM														
Occupation	*	*	*	*	*	*	*	*	.12[a]	.14[a]	.13[c]	.01	.22[c]	.02
Number of children	*	*	*	*	*	*	*	*	.09	.13[a]	*	*	.22[c]	-.04
Generation	*	*	*	*	*	*	*	*	-.15[b]	-.02	-.20[c]	-.27[c]	-.08	-.05
Feminism	*	*	*	*	*	*	*	*	*	*	.37[c]	.15[b]	.08[a]	.06
All models	*	*	*	*	*	*	*	*	.28[c]	.22[b]	.40[c]	.32[b]	.16	.16
POLITICAL INVOLVEMENT														
Occupation	.13[c]	.37[c]	.06	.22[c]	.18[c]	.22[c]	.11[a]	.28[c]	.05	.35[c]	.13[b]	.23[c]	.05	.35[c]
Number of children	*	.06	.08[a]	.08	.09	.06	-.04	.04	.02	.03	*	*	-.10[a]	-.12[a]
Generation	-.07	*	-.10[b]	-.06	-.06	-.04	.10[a]	.07	.11[a]	.07	.09	.09	.20[c]	.18[c]
Feminism	*	*	*	*	*	*	*	*	*	*	.14[b]	.05	.07	.15[c]
All models	.16[c]	.37[c]	.12	.24[b]	.19[b]	.21[b]	.21[c]	.29[c]	.21	.35[c]	.20[b]	.24[b]	.38[b]	.31[b]
POLITICAL EFFICACY														
Occupation	-.11[b]	-.20[c]	-.05	-.15[c]	-.17[c]	-.16[b]	-.10[a]	-.26[b]	.01	-.16[b]	-.12[b]	-.13[b]	-.13[b]	-.29[c]
Number of children	*	*	-.04	-.07	-.05	.01	.04	.01	.03	-.02	*	*	-.05	-.01
Generation	.02	-.01	.02	.07	.03	-.04	-.04	-.03	.05	.00	-.14[b]	-.06	.06	-.10[a]
Feminism	*	*	*	*	*	*	*	*	*	*	-.12[a]	-.03	-.06	-.14[b]
All models	.13[b]	.22[c]	.10	.18[a]	.16[a]	.17[a]	.22[c]	.28[c]	.24[b]	.18[a]	.31[b]	.25[a]	.16	.10[b]

*No data are available for these variables for these years.

Note: Figures presented are standardized regression coefficients for occupation, number of children, generation, and feminism; multiple Rs are presented for "all models," or the joint influence of all independent variables upon participation. Data concerning number of children are not available for 1952 and 1972; data concerning "feminism"(support for feminist issues) are available for 1972 and 1976 only. Positive values indicate a positive relationship between the independent and dependent variables, except for political efficacy, where negative values indicate a positive relationship.

[a] p .05.   [b] p .01.   [c] p .001.

157

women in the work force and the disparity between women's and men's wages.[20]

Second, it is surprising how little feminism explains women's participation. Given other literature, however, we cannot completely reject adherence to feminism—or support for feminist issues—as a source of women's participation. Andersen, for example, finds that feminism has increased the amount of participation among women (rather than increasing the numbers of women who participate).[21] Claire Fulenwider, using a different means of evaluating adherence to feminism, finds a positive relationship between feminism and participation in 1972 and 1976, regardless of gender.[22] Fulenwider's research, however, also supports a conclusion that feminism has a similar impact upon men's participation—which raises serious questions about the way support for feminism affects participation. Klein answers these questions by arguing that feminism affects women and men differently; women come to a support for feminism through the disjunction between their material situations and traditional expectations about women's role, while men's support of feminism is by and large an extension of their more general support for principles of equality.[23]

The strongest relationships between feminism and participation are found in 1972, and these are unique to women. For electoral activism, unconventional activism, political involvement, and feelings of political efficacy, there were significantly stronger relationships between participation and support for feminist issues among women than there were for their male equivalents. For these data and this particular year, we can speculate that two factors were present which may have caused support for feminist issues to have a particularly and uniquely positive impact upon women's participation and political attitudes. First, the feminist movement, in 1972, was still relatively new, highly visible, militant, and impressively successful. For example, the Equal Rights Amendment had been proposed in Congress that year with impressive support. This may have been the period of greatest—or at least quickest—mobilization of women in support of the movement, a mobilization which inspired and encouraged women's political activism. Second, the presidential contest in 1972 offered feminists an important outlet for political activism; the candidates, George McGovern and Richard Nixon, offered striking contrasts on a variety of issues, and McGovern was more supportive of feminist issues than was Nixon. Feminist leaders supported McGovern and were active in his campaign. In 1972, the political opportunity for feminists to engage in electoral activism was present, and this may be the explanation for the remarkably strong and unique relationships between feminism and women's electoral activism, political involvement, and political efficacy that year.

These conditions, and the feminism-activism relationship, did not obtain in 1976. However, it is still possible that, by then, feminism was having a stronger impact upon women's economic and personal lives than it was upon their political participation and that the connection between feminism and mass-level political activism is very indirect. Finally, it may also be that these questions can be addressed more successfully using other methods and other data bases; it is clear that the ICPSR surveys were not intended to provide data for intensive studies of feminism and politics.

Finally, the sources of women's political participation have not changed over time; and these sources are, for the most part, not specific to women. Occupation makes the greatest contribution to participation for both men and women, even with educational attainment controlled; however, occupation contributes more toward men's political participation than it does to women's. Occupational status is a major source of women's participation, and it is so for all forms of participation for all years. Support for feminist issues is a secondary but nonetheless important source of women's (and men's) participation. Support for feminist issues is more important to women's participation in 1972, but by 1976, it is generally more important to men's participation. Support for feminist issues is most strongly related to women's support for unconventional activism in 1972, but it is also related to women's feelings of political involvement, political efficacy, and electoral participation. Feminism is most strongly related to support for unconventional activism but is apparently independent of voting participation.

CONSIDERING THE FUTURE: CONCLUSIONS AND POSSIBILITIES

Gender related differences in mass-level political participation are not impressive—nor have they been for the years 1952 to 1976. With some few exceptions, we have found no important, unique sources of women's political activism, upon which the feminist movement might draw or which the movement might use for political mobilization of women. As is the case for men, only a relatively small proportion of women is politically active, and this holds across all groups of women— professional employees, whites, women from the middle class, and mothers, to name only a few. Given that those women who are black, from working-class family backgrounds, or employed in blue-collar occupations are among the least politically advantaged in America and that these women are not likely to see people like themselves holding political office,[24] there is reason to be pessimistic about the prospects for improving women's legal, economic, and political condition as participation among these groups of women remains low, especially in relation to other women. Claims that women's—or even feminists'— political power (in terms of women's mass-level political participation) is impressive ought, therefore, to be treated with some scepticism.

Women's electoral activism, especially in contrast to women's turn-out, is low, again especially among black and blue-collar working women. While electoral activism among men is not impressive, the implications are that men will be able to maintain an advantage in the electoral arena over women and that for both sexes, inequalities based on race, wealth, and class will persist. Men will continue to dominate the elite political arena; and white, middle-class women will continue to have electoral opportunities of which black and working-class women will not be able to take advantage. Low levels of electoral activism among women and men imply that women will not succeed in being elected to political office. Not only will female candidates not be able to rely upon significant female cadres of electoral activists (which may or may not be necessary, depending on the particular candidate and her prospective constituency), but there will be a small cohort of female activists from which to recruit candidates. Electoral activism has traditionally been a first step for women's political careers, although, of course, it has not guaranteed them. If the percentage of female electoral activists remains low, the chances for an increase in the proportion of female legislators remains low as well. Since the electoral activism of black women and blue-collar working women is low relative to other women, the chances for their needs being met also remain negligible. It is at this elite political level that gender related differences in participation are overwhelming.[25]

Another important consideration about women's political participation is the extent to which social class background and race intersect with gender to present obstacles to participation. Again, those from the working class and blacks are politically disadvantaged in the United States, for a variety of reasons. However, the ways in which a working-class background and/or being black intersect with the fact of being female may have a disproportionately disadvantageous—or perhaps only different—impact upon women's participation. The biggest differences in political participation among groups of women occur according to differences in social class background, race, and occupational status, where white-collar and blue-collar occupations are closely related to social class and race. LaFrances Rodgers-Rose's work *The Black Woman* is an example of the kind of research that is necessary to unravel the separate impact of race and sex;[26] more work of a similar nature will be required before it is clear what the political effects of social class and race are upon women—and how those effects are different, if they are, for men.

The enduring conundrum is the similarities among women's political efficacy. All women, regardless of education, class, race, or other variables, have lower levels of efficacy than do men. In addition, women's political efficacy is remarkably similar even in the face of differences in participation among groups of women and despite similarities in male and female political activism. This suggests several possibilities.

The first possibility is that the variable used to represent political efficacy measures something altogether different for women than for men. Agreement among women that ''politics and government is too complicated for someone like me to understand'' may be perceived by women as simple recognition that women are not expected to be active in or to understand politics; in this case, female respondents may be answering survey questions the way Murray Goot and Elizabeth Reid fear many do: by telling the interviewer what the respondent thinks is the gender appropriate answer.[27] Alternatively, we may interpret women's positive responses to this statement as their simple recognition of women's weak political position in the United States. If this second possibility is indeed the case, however, we still need to explain why women who believe that women have little political power are still themselves about as politically active as men.

Might there not be different sources of women's political activism than there are for men's? If feelings of political efficacy are positively related to political participation among men but not women, then perhaps a disjunction between efficacy and participation among women can be explained by other variables. We must keep in mind, however, that those other variables are not, for the most part, occupational status, number of children, feminism, or generation. Women's political participation might, however, be motivated by feelings of civic duty or stronger feelings of commitment to the community. Whatever the source of women's and men's political participation, it is not a similarly high level of political efficacy.

This prompts a second question. If women and men do have different levels of political efficacy which are not manifested in participation differences, then do efficacy differences really matter? To a certain extent, this conundrum may have little political importance. As long as women continue to participate politically, it may be of less concern that they evince less political efficacy. However, this study examines only mass political participation; it is at the elite level where gender differences are dramatic and persistent. It may be at this level that women's lower levels of efficacy have an impact: the confidence required to struggle for party nominations, to run for office, or to seek appointment to office may eliminate women from elite political involvement. Political efficacy may be especially crucial for elite political participation, given that some scholars of women's elite participation claim that women are rarely recruited for political office, that they frequently must struggle to win their party's support in a primary election, and that victory in a primary does not necessarily provide women with the same political resources that it normally provides men.[28] When Bourque and Grossholtz ask why, if women and men participate similarly on the mass level, women are not found in high public office, political efficacy may be part of the answer.[29]

This possibility leads to another explanation for women's political participation which has not been discussed thus far. Sex discrimination in politics may explain some of the gender related differences in participation which endure, especially at the elite level. Mass survey data are unlikely to yield the kind of information necessary to assess the impact of sex discrimination upon women's political participation. While it may be less likely that sex discrimination exists at, or operates with any real force at, the mass participation level, it is certainly one of the most fruitful questions for inquiry at the elite level.[30]

A second potential explanation not addressed here rests upon the differences in gender role socialization which boys and girls and, later, men and women receive. The past literature on the relationship between gender-role socialization and participation has been subjected to what can only be called scathing criticism;[31] however, M. Kent Jennings and Richard G. Niemi's studies of politics and adolescence are a useful start in correcting past scholarship.[32] Ladner, Rodgers-Rose, and others have attempted to unravel gender-role socialization according to race and class, which will also make an important contribution to understanding political socialization and its impact upon women's participation.[33] However, neither of these important possibilities can be examined using ICPSR data, which were not designed for these purposes. In general, more work on gender-role socialization is required to answer questions concerning gender-role models and participation, the process of socialization (as well as simply the agents), and how the content of gender-role socialization in "nonpolitical" areas has an impact upon political participation.[34]

Finally, findings of few or no differences between women's and men's political participation or its sources (except for political efficacy) suggest that the next important step for understanding women's political participation and for understanding its impact is an examination of the linkages (if any) between women's mass participation and women's elite participation. This would require consideration of Louis Wirth's and William Chafe's observations that women do not act as a cohesive group, politically or otherwise, because they do not see themselves as such.[35] This would also require a consideration of the successes and failures of the feminist movement, whose specific goal has been the political mobilization of women but, as this study suggests, which has not been attained in terms of widespread, mass political participation across subgroups of women. How might that mobilization best be effected, and to what extent has the feminist movement been able to mobilize women? It may be that the feminist movement's real success has been in transforming not political life—which may be in decline if participation data are the source of evidence—but in changing personal life and creating new options for women in the "private" realm.

This last question, then, of course, becomes the "larger" one, which this study has not attempted to evaluate. It is actually a series of questions regarding women's mass-level participation, but it is also a major focus of participation literature in general: why do so few women participate in politics, how can they be mobilized (or remobilized), why would we want to do so, and, finally, would it make a difference?

NOTES

1. Gabriel Almond and Sidney Verba coined the term "civic culture" to describe the type of political culture most conducive to democratic political participation. They found that the political culture of the United States most closely approximated a civic culture. See Gabriel Almond and Sidney Verba, *The Civic Culture* (Boston: Little, Brown, 1965), pp. 29–30.

2. See William Crotty, *American Parties in Decline* (Boston: Little, Brown, 1984), Table 1.1, p. 5.

3. Among many who make this argument is William Domhoff, "Why Socialists Should Be Democrats," *Socialist Revolution*, VII (1), January-February, 1977, pp. 25–36; see his exchange in the same issue with David Plotke: David Plotke, "Notes on the Democratic Party: A Rejoinder to Domhoff," pp. 37–49; and William Domhoff, "More on the Democratic Party: A Rejoinder to Plotke," pp. 51–58. For a different perspective, see Mike Davis, "The Barren Marriage of American Labour and the Democratic Party," *New Left Review*, 124, November-December 1980, pp. 43–84.

4. For information about the decline in trust the American people have in elites, see Michael Parenti, *Democracy for the Few*, 3d ed. (New York: St. Martin's Press, 1980), pp. 44–45.

5. See, for example, Norman Nie, Sidney Verba, and John R. Petrocik, *The Changing American Voter* (Cambridge, Mass.: Harvard University Press, 1976), Chapter 15.

6. See William Crotty, *Political Reform and the American Experiment* (New York: Thomas Y. Crowell, 1977), Chapter 2, especially pp. 59–60. See also Raymond E. Wolfinger and Steven J. Rosenstone, *Who Votes?* (New Haven: Yale University Press, 1980), Chapter 4. Wolfinger and Rosenstone admit that while registration requirements depress turnout, the results of electoral choice would be unchanged regardless.

7. For the extensive discussion of "pluralist" and "elitist" democratic theories, see Carole Pateman, *Participation and Democratic Theory* (Cambridge: Cambridge University Press, 1980), Chapter 1; and Michael Parenti, "Power and Pluralism: A View from the Bottom," *Journal of Politics*, XXXII (3), August 1970, pp. 501–530. See also Robert Dahl, *Who Governs?* (New Haven: Yale University Press, 1961), and *A Preface to Democratic Theory* (Chicago: University of Chicago Press, 1956); Bernard Berelson, Paul Lazarsfeld, and William McPhee, *Voting* (Chicago: University of Chicago Press, 1954), especially Chapter 23; C. Wright Mills, *The Power Elite* (New York:

Oxford University Press, 1959); T. B. Bottomore, *Elites and Society* (New York: Basic Books, 1964); and Peter Bachrach, *The Theory of Democratic Elitism: A Critique* (Boston: Little, Brown, 1967).

8. According to Antonio Gramsci, the state's legitimate use of its coercive powers rests on the acceptance of its citizens, an acceptance which is developed in civil society. As a state loses this acceptance, as civil society successfully mobilizes citizens against the state and develops a new focus for legitimacy, the state must rely increasingly upon its coercive powers to maintain itself—a reliance which becomes increasingly expensive, time consuming, and eventually hopeless. See Antonio Gramsci, *The Prison Notebooks*, ed. and trans. Quinton Hoare and Geoffrey Nowell Smith (New York: International Publishers, 1971), pp. 206–275, especially pp. 245–246.

The measure of citizenry's support for a democratic state is the extent to which citizens participate in politics and the extent to which they express satisfaction with and confidence in their chosen leaders. A combination of a decrease in voting participation and an increase in feelings of distrust, disinterest, and hostility toward the government and political parties may be an indication of a decline in legitimacy. The issue of mass participation as evidence of legitimacy, however, has been disputed. See the discussion in Pateman, *Participation and Democratic Theory*, Chapters 1 and 2, pp. 1–44; Berelson et al., *Voting*, and their acclaim of "political man" [sic] who participates occasionally; and the description of political participation and legitimacy in George Sabine, "The Two Democratic Traditions," *The Philosophical Review*, vol. 61, October 1952, pp. 451–474.

9. Note, however, that Sandra Baxter and Marjorie Lansing find that certain discrete groups of women have increased their turnout modestly from the early 1950s to 1976. See Sandra Baxter and Marjorie Lansing, *Women and Politics* (Ann Arbor: University of Michigan Press, 1984), Chapter 2.

10. Unconventional activism, measured as an attitude for the years 1968 and 1972 and as actual participation for 1976, has been excluded.

11. There are, of course, other forms of mass-level participation unexamined here due to constraints of data for which there may be uniquely "female" motivations or opportunities. See M. Kent Jennings, "Another Look at the Life Cycle and Political Participation," *American Journal of Political Science*, XXIII (4), November 1979, pp. 755–771.

12. These conclusions are drawn from data from the following tables in previous chapters: Tables 10, 13, 25, 26, 27, and 28.

13. Verba and Nie, *Participation in America*, Chapter 20, found that even when disadvantaged groups are as active as advantaged groups, they still benefit less from that activism than advantaged groups. "Participation helps those who are already better off" (p. 338). See Parenti, "Power and Pluralism," for a case study testing the claim that the needs of the disadvantaged will be "anticipated."

14. Verba and Nie, *Participation in America*, found that blacks were underrepresented in "parochial participation," the form of activism which most closely corresponds to conventional nonelectoral activity; they argue that

even controlling for social class, blacks are less likely to contact a government official than are whites. The disparity between black and white contacting behavior that remains after one has removed the effects of education, income and occupational level clearly suggests that there is indeed some racial barrier to such activity, as there is to a lesser extent with voting. Being black does not inhibit *per se* the overall activity rate of blacks—rather their social characteristics do—but it does clearly inhibit contacting government officials." (pp. 162–163)

They conclude that even "group consciousness seems unrelated to the likelihood that [a black] individual will contact the government" (pp. 163–164). Verba and Nie offer for this disparity in black-white participation the explanations that blacks believe this is a fruitless form of participation, would not know whom to contact, or never considered this particular way of solving problems (p. 167).

15. Milbrath and Goel estimate that between 1 and 5 percent of whites and between 15 and 19 percent of blacks have participated in some form of protest activity. Their 1968 Buffalo study yielded a profile of the protester: young, black, and male. See Lester W. Milbrath and M. L. Goel, *Political Participation* (Chicago: Rand McNally,1977), pp. 15 and 71.

16. Note again that the data provide responses concerning approval of unconventional activism in 1968 and 1972 and of actual unconventional participation in 1976.

17. See Bruce Campbell, *The American Electorate* (New York: Holt, Rinehart, and Winston, 1979), Table 6.1, pp. 90–91; and Nie, Verba, and Petrocik, *The Changing American Voter*, Table 15.1, p. 282.

18. See Chapter II, pp. 30–31, for a complete discussion of the political involvement variable.

19. These controls include occupational status, number of children at home, support for feminism, and, in the multivariate relationships, marital status, social class background, race, and education.

20. See the discussion in Chapter III concerning the increasing disparity between women's and men's wages for the period under study.

21. Kristi Andersen, "Working Women and Political Participation, 1952–1972," *American Journal of Political Science*, XIX (3), August 1975.

22. Claire Knoche Fulenwider, *Feminism in American Politics* (New York: Praeger, 1980), Chapter 7 and Table 7.1, p. 106.

23. See Ethel Klein, *Gender Politics* (Cambridge, Mass.: Harvard University Press, 1984), pp. 115–117.

24. On women and representation, see Virginia Sapiro's essay, "When Are Interests Interesting? The Problem of Political Representation of Women,"

American Political Science Review, 75 (3), September 1981, pp. 701–716. See also Irene Diamond and Nancy Hartsock, ''Comment'' in the same issue, pp. 717–722.

25. At this date, fewer than 5 percent of the United States House of Representatives are female, only one of whom is black; the Senate has reached a high of 2 percent female representation. Only about 8 percent of all public offices are held by women. There have been no female presidents or vice presidents, only one female Supreme Court justice, and only eleven female cabinet members in the United States history.

For a discussion of women's participation as political elites, see Jeane J. Kirkpatrick, *Political Woman* (New York: Basic Books, 1974); various essays in Part IV of Marianne Githens and Jewel L. Prestage, eds., *A Portrait of Marginality: The Political Behavior of the American Woman* (New York: Longman, 1977); Susan Tolchin and Martin Tolchin, *Clout: Womanpower and Politics* (New York: Capricorn Books, 1973); Irene Diamond, *Sex Roles in the State House* (New Haven: Yale University Press, 1977); and Ruth B. Mandel, *In the Running: The New Woman Candidate* (New Haven: Ticknor and Fields, 1981). For an excellent discussion of the barriers to women's elite participation, see Elizabeth Vallance's discussion of female candidates and nominations in the 1983 British election, ''Women Candidates in the 1983 General Election,'' *Parliamentary Affairs*, XXXVII (3), Summer 1974, pp. 301–309, where she argues that the problems of female political elites are not related to low numbers of qualified candidates but to the fact that qualified female candidates are denied nominations by parties competing in single-member constituencies. For a similar argument, based on national legislative election data for France, Italy, and the United States, see Karen Beckwith, ''Structural Barriers to Women's Access to Office: The Cases of France, Italy, and the United States,'' paper presented at the Annual Meetings of the American Political Science Association, Washington, D.C., August 30–September 2, 1984.

26. LaFrances Rodgers-Rose, ed., *The Black Woman* (Beverly Hills: Sage,1980); see also Baxter and Lansing, *Women and Politics*, Chapters Five and Six; and John C. Pierce, William P. Avery, and Addison Carey, Jr., ''Sex Differences in Black Political Beliefs and Behavior,'' *American Journal of Political Science*, XVII (2), May 1973, in regard to race and gender related differences in participation.

27. See Murray Goot and Elizabeth Reid, *Women and Voting Studies: Mindless Matrons or Sexist Scientism?* (Beverly Hills: Sage, 1975), p. 6.

28. However, keep in mind the cautions earlier in this chapter, fn. 25; success at the elite level may be completely independent of the individual ,characteristics and abilities of female candidates. See especially Tolchin and ʾTolchin, *Clout*; Vallance, ''Women Candidates''; and Beckwith, ''Structural Barriers.''

29. Susan Bourque and Jean Grossholtz, ''Politics as Unnatural Practice:

Political Science Looks at Female Participation," *Politics and Society*, IV (2), Winter 1974, p. 263.

30. See, for example, Marcia Manning Lee, "Why Few Women Hold Public Office: Democracy and Sex Roles, *Political Science Quarterly* XCI (2), 1976, p. 308, where she writes: [a] factor found to discourage women from running for office is a fear of sex discrimination."

31. See again, for example, Bourque and Grossholtz, "Politics as Unnatural Practice."

32. M. Kent Jennings and Richard G. Niemi, *The Political Character of Adolescence: The Influence of Families and Schools* (Princeton: Princeton University Press, 1974).

33. See Rodgers-Rose, *The Black Woman*; and Helen Mayer Hacker, "Class and Race Differences in Gender Roles," in Lucile Duberman, ed., *Gender and Sex in Society* (New York: Praeger, 1975), for example.

34. Virginia Sapiro, *The Political Integration of Women* (Urbana, Ill.: University of Illinois Press, 1983), makes an attempt at this; see Chapter 3.

35. See William H. Chafe, *Women and Equality: Changing Patterns in American Culture* (New York: Oxford University Press, 1977).

BIBLIOGRAPHY

Abramson, Paul R. *Generational Change in American Politics*. Lexington, Mass.: Lexington Books, 1975.

Allen, Walter R. "Family Roles, Occupational Statuses, and Achievement Orientations Among Black Women in the United States." *Signs*, IV, 4 (Summer 1979): 670–686.

Almond, Gabriel A., and Sidney Verba. *The Civic Culture: Political Attitudes and Democracy in Five Nations*. Boston: Little, Brown and Company, 1965.

American National Election Studies. Ann Arbor: Inter-University Consortium for Political and Social Research, 1952–1976.

Andersen, Kristi, "Working Women and Political Participation, 1952–1972." *American Journal of Political Science*, XIX, 3, (August 1975): 439–453.

Ascher, Carol, Louise De Salvo, and Sara Ruddick, eds. *Between Women*. Boston: Beacon Press, 1984.

Bachrach, Peter. *The Theory of Democratic Elitism: A Critique*. Boston: Little, Brown, 1967.

Ballou, Patricia K. "Review Essay: Bibliographies for Research on Women." *Signs*, III, 2 (1977): 436–450.

Baxter, Sandra, and Marjorie Lansing. *Women and Politics: The Visible Majority*. Ann Arbor: University of Michigan Press, 1983.

Beckwith, Karen. "Structural Barriers to Women's Access to Office: The Cases of France, Italy, and the United States." Paper presented at the Annual Meetings of the American Political Science Association, Washington, D.C., August 30-September 2, 1984.

Berelson, Bernard, Paul Lazarsfeld, and William McPhee. *Voting*. Chicago: University of Chicago Press, 1954.

Berman, Marshall. "Feminism, Community, Freedom." *Dissent*, Spring 1983, pp. 247–249.

Bernard, Jessie. *The Female World*. New York: The Free Press, 1981.

———. *The Future of Motherhood*. New York: Penguin, 1974.

———. *Women and the Public Interest: An Essay on Policy and Protest*. Chicago: Aldine-Atherton, 1971.

Blumberg, Paul, ed. *The Impact of Social Class*. New York: Thomas Y. Crowell, 1972.

Boals, Kay. "Review Essay: Political Science." *Signs*. I, 1 (1975): 161–174.

Boles, Janet A. *The Politics of the Equal Rights Amendment: Conflict and the Decision Process*. New York: Longman, 1979.

Bottomore, T. B. *Elites and Society*. New York: Basic Books, 1964.

Campbell, Angus, Philip E. Converse, Warren Miller, and Donald E. Stokes. *The American Voter*. New York: Wiley, 1960.

Campbell, Bruce. *The American Electorate: Attitudes and Actions*. New York: Holt, Rinehart, and Winston, 1979.

Caplan, Patricia, and Janet Bujra, eds. *Women United, Women Divided*. Bloomington, Ind.: Indiana University Press, 1980.

Carroll, Berenice A. "Review Essay: Political Science, Part I: American Politics and Political Behavior." *Signs* V, 2 (1979): 289–306.

———. "Review Essay: Political Science, Part II: International Politics, Comparative Politics, and Feminist Radicals." *Signs*, V, 3 (1980): 449–458.

Chafe, William H. *Women and Equality: Changing Patterns in American Culture*. New York: Oxford University Press, 1977.

Clarke, James. "Family Structure and Political Socialization among Urban Black Children." *American Journal of Political Science*, XVII, 2 (May 1973): 302–315.

Cloward, Richard A., and Frances Fox Piven. "Hidden Protest: The Channelling of Female Innovation and Resistance." *Signs* IV, 4 (1979): 651–669.

Crotty, William. *American Parties in Decline*. Boston: Little, Brown, 1984.

———. *Political Reform and the American Experiment*. New York: Thomas Y. Crowell, 1977.

Dahl, Robert. *A Preface to Democratic Theory*. Chicago: University of Chicago Press, 1956.

———. *Who Governs?* New Haven: Yale University Press, 1961.

Daniels, Mark R., Robert Darcy, and Joseph W. Westphal. "The ERA Won—At Least in the Opinion Polls." *PS*, XV, 4 (Fall 1982): 578–584.

Davis, Angela. "Reflections on the Black Woman's Role in the Community of Slaves." *The Black Scholar*, III, 4 (December 1971).

Dawson, Richard, and Kenneth Prewitt. *Political Socialization*. Boston: Little, Brown, 1969.

Deckard, Barbara Sinclair. *The Women's Movement: Political, Socioeconomic and Psychological Issues*. New York: Harper and Row, 1975.

Diamond, Irene. *Sex Roles in the State House*. New Haven: Yale University Press, 1977.

————, and Nancy Hartsock. "Beyond Interests in Politics: A Comment on Virginia Sapiro's 'When Are Interests Interesting? The Problem of Political Representation of Women.' " *American Political Science Review*, LXXV, 3 (September 1981): 717–721.

Dietz, Mary G. "Citizenship with a Feminist Face: The Problem with Maternal Thinking." *Political Theory*, XIII, 1 (February 1985): 19–37.

Dill, Bonnie Thornton. "The Dialectics of Black Womanhood." *Signs*, IV, 3 (1979): 543–555.

Dionne, Jr., E. J. "Pollsters Do Their Numbers on What Black America Thinks." *New York Times*, January 20, 1980.

Domhoff, William. "More on the Democratic Party: A Rejoinder to Plotke." *Socialist Revolution*, VII, 1 (January-February 1977).

————. "Why Socialists Should Be Democrats." *Socialist Revolution*, VII, 1 (January-February 1977).

Duberman, Lucile, ed. *Gender and Sex in Society*. New York: Praeger, 1975.

Duverger, Maurice. *The Political Role of Women*. Paris: UNESCO, 1955.

The Earnings Gap Between Women and Men. Washington, D.C.: U.S. Department of Labor Women's Bureau, 1979.

Ehrenreich, Barbara. "Comment on Feminism, Family and Community." *Dissent*, Winter 1983, pp. 103–106.

Eisenstein, Zillah R. "Antifeminism in the Politics and Election of 1980." *Feminist Studies*, VII, 2 (Summer 1981): 187–205.

————. *The Radical Future of Liberal Feminism*. New York: Longman, 1981.

————. "The Sexual Politics of the New Right: Understanding the 'Crisis of Liberalism' for the 1980s." In *Feminist Theory: A Critique of Ideology*, edited by Nannerl O. Keohane, Michelle Z. Rosaldo, and Barbara C. Gelpi. Chicago: University of Chicago Press, 1982.

Elshtain, Jean Bethke. "Feminism, Family, and Community." *Dissent*, Fall 1982, pp. 442–449.

————. "Reflections on War and Political Discourse." *Political Theory*, XIII, 1 (February 1985): 39–57.

Employment and Earnings: January 1981. Washington, D.C.: U.S. Department of Labor Statistics, 1981.

Evans, Judith. "The Good Society? Implications of a Greater Participation by Women in Public Life." *Political Studies*, XXXII, 4 (December 1984): 618–626.

————. "Review Article: Attitudes to Women in American Political Sci-

ence." *Government and Opposition*, XV, 1 (Winter 1980): 101–114.
———. "USA." In *The Politics of the Second Electorate: Women and Public Participation*, edited by Joni Lovenduski and Jill Hills. London: Routledge and Kegan Paul, 1981.
———. "Women and Politics: A Reappraisal." *Political Studies*, XXVIII, 2 (June 1980): 210–221.
Evans, Sara. *Personal Politics: The Roots of Women's Liberation in the Civil Rights Movement and the New Left*. New York: Knopf, 1979.
Fisher, Berenice. "The Models Among Us: Social Authority and Political Activism." *Feminist Studies*, VII, 1 (Spring 1981): 100–112.
Flammang, Janet A., ed. *Political Women: Current Roles in State and Local Government*. Beverly Hills: Sage, 1984.
Flexner, Eleanor. *Century of Struggle: The Women's Rights Movement in the United States*. Cambridge, Mass.: Belknap Press, 1975.
Freeman, Jo. *The Politics of Women's Liberation*. New York: David McKay, 1975.
Friedan, Betty. *The Feminine Mystique*. New York: Dell, 1964.
Frieze, Irene, Jacquelynne E. Parsons, Paula B.Johnson, Diane N. Ruble, and Gail L. Zellman. *Women and Sex Roles: A Social Psychological Perspective*. New York: W.W.Norton, 1978.
Fulenwider, Claire Knoche. *Feminism in American Politics: A Study of Ideological Influence*. New York: Praeger, 1980.
Giles, Micheal W., and Marilyn K. Dantico. "Political Participation and Neighborhood Social Context Revisited." *American Journal of Political Science*, XXVI, 1 (February 1982): 144–150.
Githens, Marianne, and Jewel L. Prestage, eds. *A Portrait of Marginality: The Political Behavior of the American Woman*. New York: Longman, 1977.
Goot, Murray, and Elizabeth Reid. *Women and Voting Studies: Mindless Matrons or Sexist Scientism?* Beverly Hills: Sage, 1975.
Greenstein, Fred I. *Children and Politics*. New Haven: Yale University Press, 1965.
Gurko, Miriam. *The Ladies of Seneca Falls*. New York: Schocken, 1976.
Hamilton, Richard F. *Class and Politics in the United States*. New York: Wiley, 1972.
Handbook of Women Workers. Washington, D.C.: U.S. Department of Labor Women's Bureau, 1969.
Heberle, Rudolph. *Social Movements: An Introduction to Political Sociology*. New York: Appleton-Century-Crofts, 1951.
Hill, David B. "Political Culture and Female Political Representation." *Journal of Politics*, 43 (1981): 159–168.
Hyman, Herbert H. *Political Socialization*. Glencoe, Ill.: The Free Press, 1959.

Hymowitz, Carol, and Michaele Weissman. *A History of Women in America.* New York: Bantam Books, 1978.

Jaquette, Jane S. "Introduction." In *Women in Politics*, edited by Jane S. Jaquette. New York: Wiley, 1974.

———, ed. *Women in Politics.* New York: Wiley, 1974.

Jennings, M. Kent. "Another Look at the Life Cycle and Political Participation." *American Journal of Political Science*, XXIII, 4 (November 1979): 755–771.

———, and Kenneth P. Langton. "Mothers versus Fathers: The Formation of Political Orientations Among Young Americans." *Journal of Politics*, 31 (1969): 329–358.

——— and Richard G. Niemi. "The Division of Political Labor Between Mothers and Fathers." *American Political Science Review*, LXV, 1 (March 1971): 69–82.

——— and Richard G. Niemi. *The Political Character of Adolescence: The Influence of Families and Schools.* Princeton: Princeton University Press, 1974.

——— and Norman Thomas. "Men and Women in Party Elites: Social Roles and Political Resources." *Midwest Journal of Political Science*, XII, 4 (November 1968): 469–492.

Kaplan, Temma. "Female Consciousness and Collective Action: The Case of Barcelona, 1910–1918." In *Feminist Theory: A Critique of Ideology*, edited by Nannerl O. Keohane, Michelle Z. Rosaldo, and Barbara C. Gelpi. Chicago: University of Chicago Press, 1982.

Katzenstein, Mary Fainsod. "Feminism and the Meaning of the Vote." *Signs*, X, 1 (1984): 4–26.

Kelly, Rita Mae, and Mary Boutilier. *The Making of Political Women: A Study of Socialization and Role Conflict.* Chicago: Nelson-Hall, 1978.

Keohane, Nannerl O., and Barbara C. Gelpi. "Foreward." In *Feminist Theory: A Critique of Ideology*, edited by Nannerl O. Keohane, Michelle Z. Rosaldo, and Barbara C. Gelpi. Chicago: University of Chicago Press, 1982.

Kirkpatrick, Jeane J. *The New Presidential Elite: Men and Women in National Politics.* New York: Russell Sage Foundation, 1976.

———. *Political Woman.* New York: Basic Books, 1974.

Klein, Ethel. *Gender Politics.* Cambridge, Mass.: Harvard University Press, 1984.

Knoche, Claire Fulenwider. "Political Ramifications of Feminism: A Quantitative Analysis of Participation and Alienation." Paper presented at the Annual Meetings of the American Political Science Association, Washington, D.C., September 1–4, 1977.

Koedt, Ann, and Anita Rapone, eds. *Radical Feminism*. New York: Quadran-
    gle, 1972.

Kohn, Melvin L. *Class and Conformity: A Study in Values*. Homewood, Ill.:
    Dorsey, 1969.

Komarovsky, Mirra. *Blue-Collar Marriage*. New York: Vintage, 1967.

————. *Women's Role in Contemporary Society*. New York: Avon, 1972.

Kraditor, Aileen. *The Ideas of the Women's Suffrage Movement, 1890–1920*.
    New York: Anchor, 1971.

Krauss, Wilma Rule. "Political Implications of Gender Roles: A Review of
    the Literature." *American Political Science Review*, LXVIII (4), De-
    cember 1974, pp. 1706–1723.

Langton, Kenneth. *Political Socialization*. New York: Oxford University Press,
    1969.

Lazarsfeld, Paul, Bernard Berelson, and Hazel Gaudet. *The People's Choice*.
    New York: Columbia University Press, 1968.

Lee, Marcia Manning. "Why Few Women Hold Public Office: Democracy
    and Sex Roles, *Political Science Quarterly*, XCI (2), Summer 1976,
    297-314.

Lerner, Gerda. *The Majority Finds Its Past*. New York: Oxford University
    Press, 1979.

Levine, Murray. "Method or Madness: On the Alienation of the Profes-
    sional." Paper presented at the Annual Meetings of the American Psy-
    chological Association, Montreal, September 1–5, 1980.

Lewis, Diane K. "A Response to Inequality: Black Women, Racism and Sex-
    ism." *Signs*, III, 2 (1977): 339–361.

Lopata, Helena Z. *Occupation: Housewife*. London: Oxford University Press,
    1971.

————, and Barrie Thorne. "On the Term 'Sex Roles.' " *Signs*, III, 3 (Spring
    1978): 718–721.

Lovenduski, Joni, and Jill Hills, eds. *The Politics of the Second Electorate:
    Women and Public Participation*. London: Routledge and Kegan Paul,
    1981.

McDonagh, Eileen L. "To Work or Not To Work: The Differential Impact of
    Achieved and Derived Status upon the Political Participation of Women,
    1956–1976." *American Journal of Political Science*, XXVI, 2 (May
    1982): 280–297.

McKinley, Donald Gilbert. *Social Class and Family Life*. London: The Free
    Press, 1964.

Mandel, Ruth B. *In the Running: The New Woman Candidate*. New Haven:
    Ticknor and Fields, 1981.

Mannheim, Karl. *Essays on the Sociology of Knowledge*. London: Routledge
    and Kegan Paul, 1952.

Milbrath, Lester W., and M. L. Goel. *Political Participation*. Chicago: Rand McNally, 1977.

Miller, Arthur H., Patricia Gurin, Gerald Gurin, and Oksana Malanchuk. "Group Consciousness and Political Participation." *American Journal of Political Science*, XXV, 3 (August 1981).

Mills, C. Wright. *The Power Elite*. New York: Oxford University Press, 1959.

Moynihan, Daniel P. *The Negro Family: The Case for National Action*. Washington, D.C.: U.S. Department of Labor, 1965.

Nie, Norman H., Sidney Verba, and John R. Petrocik. *The Changing American Voter*. Cambridge, Mass: Harvard University Press, 1976.

O'Leary, Virginia E. *Toward Understanding Women*. Monterey, Calif.: Brooks/Cole, 1977.

O'Neill, William L. *Everyone Was Brave: The Rise and Fall of Feminism in America*. Chicago: Quadrangle, 1969.

Papanek, Hanna. "Family Status Production: The 'Work' and 'Non-Work' of Women." *Signs* IV, 4 (1979): 775–781.

Parenti, Michael. *Democracy for the Few*. New York: St. Martin's Press, 1980.

———. "Power and Pluralism: A View from the Bottom." *Journal of Politics*, XXXII, 3 (August 1970).

Pateman, Carole. *Participation and Democratic Theory*. Cambridge: Cambridge University Press, 1970.

Peattie, Lisa, and Martin Rein. *Women's Claims: A Study in Political Economy*. Oxford: Oxford University Press, 1983.

Pierce, John C., William P. Avery, and Addison Carey, Jr. "Sex Differences in Black Political Beliefs and Behavior." *American Journal of Political Science*, XVII, 2 (May 1973): 422–430.

Piven, Frances Fox, and Richard Cloward. *Poor People's Movements*. New York: Vintage, 1979.

Plotke, David. "Notes on the Democratic Party: A Response to Domhoff." *Socialist Revolution*, VII, 1 (January-February 1977).

Randall, Vicky. *Women and Politics*. New York: St. Martin's Press, 1982.

Rapoport, Ronald B. "The Sex Gap in Political Persuading: Where the 'Structuring Principle' Works." *American Journal of Political Science*, XXV, 1 (February 1981): 32–48.

Redstockings, eds. *Feminist Revolution: An Abridged Edition*. New York: Random House, 1978.

Richmond-Abbott, Marie. *Masculine and Feminine: Sex Roles over the Life Cycle*. Reading, Mass.: Addison-Wesley, 1983.

Rodgers, Harrell R., and Michael Harrington. *Unfinished Democracy*. Glenview, Ill.: Scott, Foresman, 1981.

Rodgers-Rose, LaFrances, ed. *The Black Woman*. Beverly Hills: Sage, 1980.

Rosaldo, M. Z. "The Use and Abuse of Anthropology: Reflections on Feminism and Cross-Cultural Understanding." *Signs*, V, 3 (1980): 389–417.

Rowbotham, Sheila. *Woman's Consciousness, Man's World*. Middlesex, Eng.: Penguin, 1973.

Sabine, George. "The Two Democratic Traditions." *The Philosophical Review*, 61 (October 1952).

Salper, Roberta, ed. *Female Liberation*. New York: Knopf, 1972.

Samuels, Richard J., ed. *Political Generations and Political Development*. Lexington, Mass.: Lexington Books, 1977.

Sapiro, Virginia. *The Political Integration of Women*. Urbana, Ill.: University of Illinois Press, 1983.

———."Private Costs of Public Commitments or Public Costs of Private Commitments? Family Roles verus Political Ambition." *American Journal of Political Science*, XXVI, 2 (May 1982): 265–279.

———. "When Are Interests Interesting? The Problem of Political Representation of Women." *American Political Science Review*, 75, 3 (September 1981).

Sayers, Dorothy L. *Gaudy Night*. New York: Harper and Row, 1936.

Secombe, Wally. "The Housewife and Her Labour Under Capitalism." *New Left Review*, 83 (January-February 1973).

Shingles, Richard D. "Black Consciousness and Political Participation: The Missing Link." *American Political Science Review*, LXXV, 1 (March 1981): 76–91.

Sochen, June, ed. *The New Feminisms in Twentieth-Century America*. Lexington, Mass.: D. C. Heath, 1971.

Stambler, Sookie, ed. *Women's Liberation: A Blueprint for the Future*. New York: Ace Books, 1970.

A Statistical Portrait of Women in the U.S. U.S. Department of Commerce, Bureau of the Census. Washington, D.C.: General Printing Office, 1976.

Tanner, Leslie B., ed. *Voices from Women's Liberation*. New York: Mentor, 1970.

Thomas, John Clayton. "Citizen-Initiated Contacts with Government Agencies: A Test of Three Theories." *American Journal of Political Science*, XXVI, 3 (August 1983): 504–522.

Thompson, Mary Lou, ed. *Voices of the New Feminism*. Boston: Beacon Press, 1970.

Tolchin, Susan, and Martin Tolchin. *Clout: Womanpower and Politics*. New York: Capricorn Books, 1976.

Vallance, Elizabeth. "Women Candidates in the 1983 General Election." *Parliamentary Affairs*, XXXVII, 3 (Summer 1984): 301–309.

Vanek, Joann. "Time Spent in Housework." *Scientific American*, 231, 5 (November 1974).

Verba, Sidney, and Norman H. Nie. *Participation in America: Political Democracy and Social Equality*. New York: Harper and Row, 1972.
————, and Jae-On Kim. *Participation and Political Equality: A Seven-Nation Comparison*. Cambridge: Cambridge University Press, 1978.
Wallace, Michelle. *Black Macho and the Myth of the Superwoman*. New York: Dial, 1978.
Welch, Susan. "Women as Political Animals? A Test of Some Explanations for Male-Female Political Participation Differences."*American Journal of Political Science*, XXI, 4 (November 1977): 711–730.
Wolfinger, Raymond E., and Steven J. Rosenstone. *Who Votes?* New Haven: Yale University Press, 1980.

INDEX

participation (white-collar and
blue-collar), 43–44, 48; profes-
sionally-employed women, 152–
53; women, blue-collar, 45, 47–
48, 152–53, 160; women, white-
collar, 45, 47, 150; women, in the
labor force, 36. *See also* Occupation; Occupational status

ABOUT THE AUTHOR

KAREN BECKWITH is Assistant Professor of Political Science at the College of Wooster in Wooster, Ohio. She has done extensive research on women's electoral representation and policy issues in both Italy and the United States, and is the author of numerous articles and conference papers. She is an Associate Editor of the journal *Women and Politics*.